FEEDBACK FUNDAMENTALS AND EVIDENCE-BASED BEST PRACTICES

D0165384

Feedback is an incredibly valuable source of information – it enables us to be more self-aware and understand what we are doing well, and it tells us what we could be doing differently, more of, or less of to improve our performance and achieve our goals. *Feedback Fundamentals and Evidence-Based Best Practices: Give It, Ask for It, Use It* provides an essential overview of feedback fundamentals, what gets in the way of effective feedback exchanges, and the impact of technology on feedback interactions.

The value of feedback is often unrealized because people dread giving it, dread receiving it, and may not know what to do with it once they get it. *Feedback Fundamentals and Evidence-Based Best Practices* balances research, testimonials, and practical tools to provide readers with a thorough understanding of feedback exchanges. Critical findings from decades of research in psychology, business, and other disciplines are distilled into tools and strategies that readers can easily adopt in their own lives, regardless of who they are or what they do. Throughout the book are a wealth of examples from a variety of people and situations, both within and outside traditional work contexts.

Feedback Fundamentals and Evidence-Based Best Practices: Give It, Ask for It, Use It is a crucial resource for professionals, leaders, and anyone of any industry or stage in life looking to give better feedback, proactively ask for feedback, gracefully receive feedback, and put that feedback to use.

Brodie Gregory Riordan, PhD, is an industrial/organizational psychologist focused on helping people unlock their potential through coaching, feedback, goal setting, and other best practices from psychological science. Her career has included global roles in learning, leadership development, and talent management with Procter & Gamble, CEB (Corporate Executive Board), and McKinsey & Company. Brodie has also published under her maiden name, Jane Brodie Gregory.

"Listening to what the universe tells us about how we perform, the results we create, and the general way we impact the world is one of the most important and difficult things we do as people. Riordan provides a fantastic viewpoint of how to think about feedback that is around us at all times and participate as feedback givers and receivers every day. Her practical, science-based approach to this topic applies to everyone, whether a student, early career professional, manager, or a leader – if you have a pulse and want to improve your life, this book will give you insight into how to do that."

Rich Cober, Chief HR Officer, USA

"This book is a gift to anyone looking to reach their goals both personally and professionally by harnessing the power of feedback. Feedback is all around us in our daily lives. Feedback can propel you forward if you are open to owning how it impacts you as both the giver and receiver. In my work, feedback is something that can be the difference maker in driving a productive company culture or turning it into a toxic one. This book provides easy-to-implement strategies for how to have thoughtful and constructive conversations regarding feedback, which in turn empowers individuals to be the best version of themselves."

Emily Roberts, President of a corporate wellness company, USA

"Feedback is to growth as growth is to success. This book inexorably links the necessity of both positive and negative feedback with unlocking life's full potential. The concept of using feedback as a forward-looking message has been transformational for me as I continue to grow my team and manage their professional potential. I will continue to refer to this book as I grow in my role as a leader in my company."

Matthew Coursen, Executive Managing Director at JLL, USA

FEEDBACK FUNDAMENTALS AND EVIDENCE-BASED BEST PRACTICES

Give It, Ask for It, Use It

BRODIE GREGORY RIORDAN

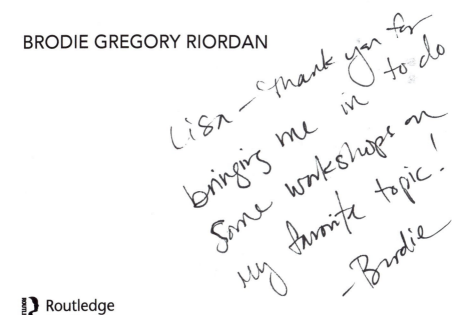

Lisa – thank you for bringing me in to do some workshops on my favorite topic!
–Brodie

Routledge
Taylor & Francis Group

NEW YORK AND LONDON

First published 2021
by Routledge
52 Vanderbilt Avenue, New York, NY 10017

and by Routledge
2 Park Square, Milton Park, Abingdon, Oxon, OX14 4RN

Routledge is an imprint of the Taylor & Francis Group, an informa business

© 2021 Taylor & Francis

Library of Congress Cataloging-in-Publication Data
Names: Riordan, Brodie Gregory, author.
Title: Feedback fundamentals and evidence-based best practices : give it, ask for it, use it / Brodie Gregory Riordan.
Description: New York, NY : Routledge, 2021. | Includes bibliographical references and index.
Identifiers: LCCN 2020014798 (print) | LCCN 2020014799 (ebook) | ISBN 9780367344122 (hardback) | ISBN 9780367344139 (paperback) | ISBN 9780429325656 (ebook)
Subjects: LCSH: Feedback (Psychology)
Classification: LCC BF319.5.F4 R56 2021 (print) | LCC BF319.5.F4 (ebook) | DDC 158.7—dc23
LC record available at https://lccn.loc.gov/2020014798
LC ebook record available at https://lccn.loc.gov/2020014799

ISBN: 978-0-367-34412-2 (hbk)
ISBN: 978-0-367-34413-9 (pbk)
ISBN: 978-0-429-32565-6 (ebk)

Typeset in Adobe Garamond Pro and Avenir
by Swales & Willis, Exeter, Devon, UK

CONTENTS

ACKNOWLEDGMENTS

I am deeply grateful for the opportunity to write this book about a topic that only gets more interesting, relevant, and meaningful to me with time. Thank you to Christina Chronister, Veronica Morgan, Danielle Dyal, and Molly Selby at Routledge/Taylor & Francis for this opportunity and the support along the way.

Thank you to, Adam, Alex, Christopher, David, Finch, Frances, Goodloe, Justice, Nia, and Parker for participating in interviews for this book. Their great examples brought the content to life and hopefully provided every reader with a scenario they could relate to.

Kristen Wong Van Hise, thank you for translating my rough mock-ups of figures into sketches that turn complex ideas about feedback into clear, logical processes and lists.

Paul Levy, thank you for igniting my interest in this topic and for all of the learning, guidance, mentoring, support, and collaboration over the years, and for reading early drafts of this book and providing feedback on feedback!

Ariel Roberts, thank you for being an extraordinary feedback thought-partner, for helping me with early research, and providing detailed feedback that helped me shape the final draft. Thank you to Ali O'Malley, Blair Hixson Davis, Jennifer Porter, and Kate Johnson for providing feedback on drafts along the way.

And, most of all, thank you to my husband, Tim Riordan, my parents, Helen and Ted Gregory, and my sister, Lane Gregory, for hearing and reading so much about feedback, all the time, and always remaining patient and helping me shape and streamline my ideas!

PART I

FEEDBACK
FUNDAMENTALS

CHAPTER 1

WHY FEEDBACK MATTERS

I give feedback that is honest and direct. I focus on people's actions in specific situations. I emphasize my feelings, the impact on me. I think my honesty about what I'm seeing and feeling makes it constructive. I try to make it forward looking – "Next time you might handle it this way."

Christopher, alumni member of Back on My Feet

It's easy to associate the word "feedback" with formal experiences, like an annual performance review or a customer feedback survey. But actually, feedback is all around us, all the time. We get feedback from others, from our environment, even from our own observations and inner monologue. Giving and receiving feedback are dynamic experiences that shape and are shaped by our relationships and the context of the conversation.

The purpose of this book is to illuminate the value of feedback, the many shapes that feedback can assume, and just how often we are immersed in feedback in our day-to-day lives. My hope is that by the time you finish this book you understand, value, and appreciate feedback a little more, see feedback from a different perspective than you did before you started the book, and find giving, receiving, asking for, and using feedback a little easier. This book is intended for anyone and everyone who deals with feedback. Which is pretty much *everyone*. It draws on a wealth of research findings about what makes feedback work and what gets in the way, and presents these findings in a way that will enable you apply them in your life and work right away.

Nearly two decades ago, in the early months of my PhD program, I met with my PhD advisor to talk about what I would focus on in my thesis and ongoing research. When he told me that his research focused largely on feedback, I thought to myself, "OMG that is so boring. How can you spend your entire career studying something as dull and specific as *feedback?*" Clearly, as time went on, I saw the light and became his feedback-studying protégé. What I initially considered a dry, dull, transactional exchange gradually evolved into a rich, complex, and important human interaction. Over the years, I've come to appreciate just how prevalent feedback is, what a difference it can make in people's lives, and how little most people know about the feedback best practices that we've learned from decades of research in psychology, business, and other disciplines. We often talk about feedback in the context of work, but, in actuality, feedback impacts relationships and interactions in all parts of our lives.

I am intrigued by people's feedback behavior both inside and outside of work. *Why does this colleague get so twitchy and nervous when people give him even the most basic feedback? Why did that manager just give her team member tough feedback in the middle of the company kitchen where everyone could hear? Why would people rather disregard useful feedback than embrace their opportunities to grow?* It's easy to over-index on formal and uncomfortable feedback events, like performance reviews, but, in reality, we are immersed in feedback of all shapes and sizes, all day, every day. To get a better sense of just how much feedback I encounter on a day-to-day basis, I decided to pay close attention to the number of times I had a feedback "event" on a typical day. At the end of the day I had given, asked for, received, or used feedback 25 times (and I probably missed a few!).

The morning started with a few data points that led to some self-generated feedback (among others):

1. I was still tired when I woke up and needed caffeine to get going, which was important feedback that I need to be more disciplined about going to bed on time (*received*)
2. On my morning run my tight hamstrings were feedback that I've been sitting too much lately (*received*)
3. I asked my husband if my outfit looked okay, he suggested a plain blue blazer would look better than the patterned one I had on; I agreed and then changed blazers (*asked, received, used*)
4. The chill I felt when I left for work told me I needed a heavier coat and that I should remember to check the weather before I leave the house (*received*)

5. The countdown on the "walk" sign told me I needed to hurry up if I wanted to cross the street before the light changed (*received*)
6. I told the coffee shop barista that my café Cubano was a little too sweet for "medium sweet" (*gave*)

Once my workday started the feedback was more likely to involve other people, and technology played a significant role throughout:

7. The 75 new emails in my inbox told me I should have checked my email one last time the night before (*received*)
8. On a team call, three colleagues shared helpful suggestions on a document we were developing, which informed my next round of revisions later that day (*received and used*)
9. I asked a colleague for his candid reactions to a website my team is developing, and he shared a variety of positive comments and opportunities to make the website more tailored to the needs and preferences of our end users (*asked and received*)
10. I asked a few colleagues to weigh in on a budget proposal and share their feedback on where and how certain allocations are being made (*asked*)
11. A colleague told me that a recent survey I sent out lacked a "Not Applicable" option, which made it hard to respond to some items (*received*)
12. An instant message from a colleague told me that I was 9 minutes late to a conference call (*received*)
13. My sister texted me to ask me to weigh in on how she handled a recent conversation she had with our parents (*gave, in response to being asked*)
14. A colleague suggested I reconsider bringing paper handouts to a conference that aspired to be paperless (*received*)
15. A designer shared an updated concept of a visual document and I provided her with a few changes to make in the next round (*gave*)
16. I used an online feedback tool to formally recognize four colleagues for the great work they did launching a program that touched 16,000 users (*gave*)
17. A team member asked for feedback on a document for our leadership team; I told her what was strong and high impact about the document, shared two specific recommendations for enhancements, and thanked her for taking the lead on it (*gave, in response to being asked*)

And the feedback continued into the evening:

18. My yoga teacher asked for feedback on a new sequence of poses and her new playlist; I told her the sequence was very challenging and that the tone and

tempo of the playlist was a great match to the sequence (*gave, in response to being asked*)

19. The director of a nonprofit whose board I'm on apologized for taking a few hours to send me a document, and I told her that there was no hurry and her timing was fine (*gave*)

20. I commented on my niece's Instagram post, to let her know how much I liked her picture (*gave*)

21. I read Yelp reviews of the two restaurants I was considering for dinner and made a choice largely based on other users' reviews and photos (*used*)

22. I sent my mother-in-law a note letting her know how much I appreciated her calling me the week that my grandmother had died, and that our conversation had helped me process my emotions (*gave*)

23. I weighed in on a few options for my father's birthday dinner, taking into consideration his preference for steak, down-to-earth authentic places, and not too much noise (*gave*)

24. My husband told me that he wished I didn't have work calls at 9:30pm on a Thursday, because Thursday nights are for relaxing (*received*)

25. At 1am I knocked on our neighbor's wall to let him know that it was a little late to show off his impressive sound system (*gave*)

What's interesting to me about this random sample of feedback is that most of it is positive or neutral – not particularly negative or critical. Most of my experiences were also so mundane and routine that they could easily be overlooked as feedback experiences. Out of all the 25 feedback events in my day, none triggered a strong emotional reaction, nothing insulted me or hurt my feelings, and none resulted in inconvenience or major changes in direction for whatever I was working on. Contrast this with my recent nonscientific survey: I asked 154 people about their immediate reaction when they hear the word "feedback" or "let me give you some feedback" – 67% reacted in a decidedly negative way. For example:

- "No specific words come to mind but I get this feeling in my body – like I raise and tighten my shoulders, I feel like I'm bristling."
- "My first instinct is, 'I wonder what I did wrong!'"
- "Yikes! Duck and wait for criticism."
- "Brace yourself!"
- "Ugh!" (this specific reaction was cited by six people!)
- "Poker face now!"
- "Sweaty palms, racing heart, fake smile, '"sure, I'd love to hear it!'"
- "I steel myself to hear something negative. Rarely hear positivity wrapped up in 'feedback.'"
- "I overthink it and my anxiety hits the roof even though I know feedback is a gift."

Some described their reaction as an almost Pavlovian[1] response. Simply hearing the word "feedback" provokes an instant physical and emotional reaction. Feedback is clearly a powerful word and loaded with baggage from unpleasant past experiences if it can elicit that kind of immediate response. However, feedback is an extraordinarily useful source of information. It helps people be more self-aware, gauge progress toward goals, know what they are doing well and should keep doing, and identify things that they might want to do differently. Feedback provides the information necessary to perform at a higher level, achieve goals, grow, and have deeper self-understanding. But for people who actively dislike feedback and dread receiving it, that value is lost.

How did we get to this point? People are not born dreading feedback – it's a learned response. Most of the feedback we receive is nonthreatening and helps us to navigate the world around us, our relationships, and our social interactions, and to stay on track with our work, life, and personal goals. I suspect that most of the feedback we receive on a day-to-day basis doesn't even register as "feedback." Somehow, the word has come to connote a harsh, painful, sometimes unfair dumping of information that is outside of our control.

For people who have had just enough unpleasant feedback exchanges that elicit a strong emotional response and that have become deeply engrained in their memories, their orientation toward feedback plummets. Every person has a *feedback orientation* that underlies how they think about, feel about, and are motivated to use feedback (Linderbaum & Levy, 2010). That orientation is shaped largely by our past experiences with feedback, for better or for worse.

Feedback orientation is disproportionately influenced by the teachers, coaches, parents, bosses, and colleagues who give us feedback over the course of our lives, many of whom are just as uncomfortable providing feedback as they are receiving it. Negative feedback – that which identifies gaps between our goals and our current performance – provides some of the most useful information, but is often disliked and avoided. It tells us exactly what we need to do to close the gap between where we are and where we want to be. Negative feedback is often misconstrued as "feedback given poorly" and therefore referred to instead by less daunting names like "constructive feedback" (really, ALL feedback should be constructive. Why would you ever give *unconstructive* feedback?). **The word "negative" simply means the feedback highlights a deficit, or gap, between our goals and our current state**. When faced with providing negative feedback, people are likely to stall, avoid giving it, or provide it in a way that is so diluted or sandwiched between positive feedback that people are left completely unclear as to what the real issue is, why it matters, and what they should do about it. This discomfort providing negative feedback results in a loss for everyone involved. The person providing the feedback misses an opportunity to share their valuable perspective, help another person grow and improve, and potentially highlight a blind spot for that person. The person who would be the target of the feedback misses out on valuable information that would help them better understand their current level of performance, and how close or far that current performance is from their goals. Without negative feedback we are blind to what we need to do better or to how we can close in on our goals.

Are Goals without Feedback Goals at All?

If a tree falls in the woods and no one is there to hear it, does it make a sound? More importantly, without feedback on our goals how do we know how we're tracking against those goals? Our behavior is driven by goals. Sometimes those goals are explicit – those that we deliberately set, actively track, and maybe even share with others. But many of our goals are implicit. Perhaps the reason you brush your teeth at night is to have good dental health, to avoid a trip to the dentist, or to have fresher breath. Whatever your goal, you probably don't actively think about it every night, yet it drives you to brush your teeth every evening. Anytime we are motivated to do something, a goal is driving that behavior.

Our progress toward attaining goals depends on feedback. Feedback tells us where we stand in relation to goals, expectations, and standards. It comes from other people, our environment (e.g., your scale or car speedometer), our bodies (pain, hunger, discomfort, etc.), and our own inner monologue. Feedback helps us to gauge where we stand in pursuit of our goals and the things that are important to us and, as a result, serves an important motivating (or demotivating) function. As we work toward achieving our goals, the closer we get, the more motivated and inspired we are to press on. A lack of progress against goals, despite our best efforts, can deflate and demotivate. Making progress more rapidly than anticipated may inspire us to revise our goals to be more challenging (Locke & Latham, 2002). But, without feedback, our efforts to achieve goals occur in a vacuum. We lack visibility into how close or far we are from attaining our goals and, therefore, if our level of effort is appropriate, too little, or too great. For example, if your goal is to run a marathon in 4 hours but you have no mechanism for assessing how far you have run or how much time has elapsed, your goal is meaningless and your efforts will feel fruitless. Without feedback

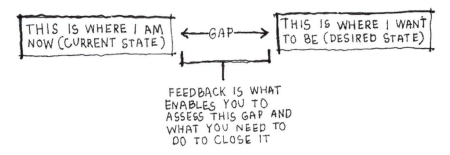

Figure 1.1 Feedback tells you the gap between where you are now and where you want to be.

on your progress you won't know if your pace is on track, too slow, or too fast. Feedback provides critical data that empower us to self-regulate our behavior, our effort, and even our expectations.

Feedback enables increased self-awareness, tells us exactly what we need to do to have higher performance or be better at just about anything, and can fuel growth and development. Negative feedback – that which highlights a gap between where we are and where we want to be – can also tell us exactly what we need to do to close that gap. This deficit tells us what we need to learn, how we need to change our behavior, and what we need to do more of, less of, or differently to achieve our goal.

Positive feedback lets us know what we are doing well, that we have met our goal or expectations, and that we might be able to slow down our efforts or keep doing the right things that are working for us. Without feedback we would be adrift in a world with little context or direction. Imagine a world where you had no idea how you were doing in school, in your job performance, your marriage; where you didn't know how others perceived you and what they found lovely or recalcitrant about you. Our work, relationships, and sense of self would all suffer in a world devoid of feedback.

Sort of like a Thermostat

Feedback and goals work together in a way that is similar to a thermostat in your home. You set a desired temperature on your thermostat, and the heater or air conditioner responds by sensing the current room temperature and acting accordingly to close the gap between the current temperature and the desired temperature. This is a basic control loop – and that's exactly how feedback operates in conjunction with our goals or expectations. In any given situation, a person has a desired state – a goal, something they are trying to achieve or maintain. The goal or standard can be explicit – something that the person has really thought about and articulated – or implicit – an assumed goal or expectation. In most situations, there is a gap between that desired state and the current state, and the only way to assess that gap is through feedback.

One example most people can relate to is weight. Say your goal weight is 150 pounds. When you step on the scale you receive immediate feedback that tells you where you stand with respect to your goal – the distance between the current state versus the desired state. The direction of that gap varies. If you weigh 160 pounds then the scale is giving you negative feedback – telling you that you are 10 pounds short of your desired state. In this instance, when a gap is highlighted, the feedback is *negative*. However, if you have been trying to lose weight and weigh in at 140 pounds, then the scale offers *positive* feedback – you have exceeded your goal by 10 pounds. Negative feedback simply indicates a gap between where you are and where you want to be; positive feedback shows that you have met or exceeded your goal (there is no gap or deficit).

Control theory is a theory of motivation that suggests that we are motivated to achieve goals, and that our ability to assess the distance between our current state and our desired goal state fuels us to act (Carver & Scheier, 1998). Control theory provides a structured framework for thinking about feedback in any context. Any goal, project, or aspiration that you have can be mapped to control theory. Think about a goal you have right now – can you map it to a basic control loop? What is your current state? What is your goal? When you compare those two, what feedback are you generating about the distance between your current and desired state, and how you can close that gap?

Here's an example of a control loop applied to career growth. Whitney is currently a senior manager in the finance group at her organization (current state). She wants to be a director in the group (goal/desired state). She uses indirect and direct sources of feedback to help her know where she stands in her pursuit of this goal:

- Indirect: There is an open director position in her group and she believes that she meets the qualifications based on the job posting and her experience
- Direct: Her manager tells her that she has fully mastered her current role and should be thinking about what's next for her

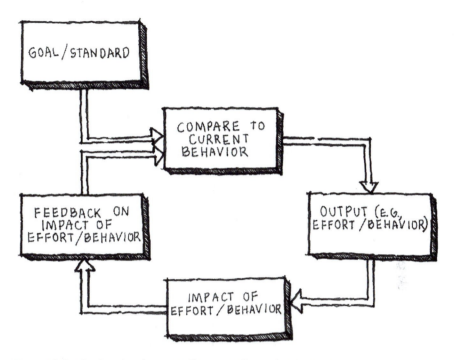

Figure 1.2 Feedback and goals operate like a control loop – just like the thermostat in your house. (Adapted from Carver & Scheier, 1998).

Based on these data points, Whitney believes that she is very close to closing the gap between her current state and her goal of moving into the director role. She feels energized and excited by the momentum and takes any action that is within her control to close the gap (updating her resume, letting her manager know that she is interested in the role, reaching out to the hiring manager, officially applying for the job). In this example, the feedback Whitney receives indicates that she is closing in on achieving her goal.

As people get closer to their goal, they can experience a spike in motivation, encouraging them through the final push. On the other hand, if feedback indicates that progress is going in the WRONG direction, and they are getting further from their goal, it's common to feel a drop in motivation. For instance, if Whitney had discovered that the director role was going away and the next step in her career was a vice president role, for which she wouldn't be qualified for a few more years, she would likely feel "demotivated" – losing energy, momentum, and motivation to push toward that next step, since the gap between her current and desired state is now larger than she expected. Thus, the feedback we receive plays an important role in our level of motivation, helping us gauge the distance between our current state and our aspirations. When feedback indicates that we are closing in on our goal, we feel a fresh surge of motivation. When feedback is discouraging and tells us that the gap is bigger than we expected, that sinking sense of demotivation sets in.

Feedback Intervention Theory (FIT; Kluger & DeNisi, 1996) builds on control theory with some important distinctions. FIT suggests that people regulate their behavior and gain self-awareness by comparing feedback about their current behavior to some set of standards or expectations (like the goal or standard in control theory). These expectations or standards can be self-generated or can come from someone else, such as a boss, a partner, a parent, etc. When we detect a discrepancy between our current behavior and the standard or expectation, we are motivated to change our behavior and close the gap. Receiving feedback on that specific behavior directs our attention toward the behavior, which increases the likelihood that we'll notice what we need to change (self-awareness), and then reflect the change in future behavior.

When it comes to standards, our default is to compare our behavior and feedback against *our own* standards, rather than others' standards. Challenges arise when those standards (ours versus others') don't align. For example, you and your kids have different standards about what it means for a room to be "clean." You and your boss have two different interpretations of a particular performance expectation. One tenet of classic goal setting theory is that challenging and specific goals are most effective for driving high performance. One of the *worst* goals you can set is to simply "do your best" (Locke & Latham, 2002). "Do your best" goals do not drive high performance because they lack specificity about what "best" looks like and also lack the necessary level of challenge that stretches people to higher performance. In the context of FIT, "do your best" goals are ineffective because they create vague standards. If your boss tells you to "do your best," her expectation of "your best" may not be the same as your own, leading to a disconnect in expectations. Specificity is key for effective goal, standard, and expectation setting, as well as giving the feedback that helps us to track our progress against those standards.

Standards come in different levels of abstraction, in a hierarchy from broad and overarching to very specific. For example, at the top of your personal standards' hierarchy may be an expectation of being a "good person." At the opposite end of the hierarchy are all of the specific, micro behaviors that ultimately add up to being a good person. When it comes to regulating our behavior, we focus on the middle level of abstraction or hierarchy. Like Goldilocks and the Three Bears, we struggle to act when feedback or standards are either too high-level or too micro. When feedback and standards are too high-level, they lack the specificity for us to translate them into specific actions and behaviors. However, going too low on the hierarchy and focusing at the micro-action level can be inefficient and demand significant cognitive resources. Feedback and standards in the middle are just right – they offer enough clarity and specificity for us to adjust our behavior in meaningful ways without too much cognitive effort.

All Feedback Consists of Four Elements

Feedback can feel intimidating and emotionally charged. But when we break it down into its core elements, even the most challenging feedback discussion can feel a little less intimidating. Recognizing the building blocks of feedback and where things could derail (Is it what I said? How I said it? When I said it? The other person's attitude? My own incompetence?) diminishes some of the risk and uncertainty of both giving and receiving feedback. Every feedback exchange – no matter who is involved, how minor or serious the topic, positive or negative – consists of four elements: The feedback provider ("source"), the actual message, the context in which it is provided, and the perceptions and attitudes of the recipient (Gregory & Levy, 2015). In other words, who is giving the feedback, what are they saying, where/when are they providing it, and to whom? This sounds simple enough, but a deeper look at each of these four elements reveals important nuances that impact the effectiveness of the feedback exchange. The ultimate goals of feedback are to help people become more self-aware, to grow and develop, and to do more of something, less of something,

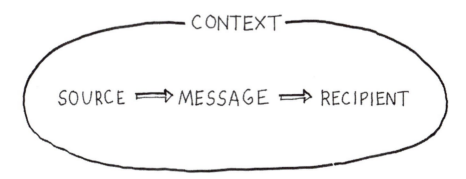

Figure 1.3 All feedback exchanges consist of four elements

[2] (Gregory & Levy, 2015).

or something altogether different in the future. Achieving these goals depends on whether or not someone will accept the feedback in the first place. All four elements of the model in Figure 1.3 impact the likelihood that someone will accept and use feedback.

Source. All feedback comes from someone or something. As we saw earlier in the chapter, much of the feedback we process throughout the day is self-generated or comes from our environment. But the feedback that tends to stand out most and, at times, feel both most fulfilling or most emotionally challenging, is the feedback that comes from other people. And not all feedback providers are created equal! Attributes of feedback providers, as well as our history and relationships with them, influence our perceptions of their feedback.

Research has consistently shown that feedback is most likely to be accepted and put to use when the person providing it is perceived to be credible – that they are trustworthy and have some expertise on the topic at hand (Ilgen, Fisher, & Taylor, 1979). In other words, the recipient trusts them and thinks that they know what they are talking about. For example, David, a Grammy-winning musician and producer, notes that critical feedback from a credible source with great experience and a great ear goes a really long way, whereas feedback from someone whose opinion you disagree with can send another message entirely.

Says David,

> A really good producer can effectively give constructive feedback – including hard truths. It's easy to be a "yes man" and just tell people they are brilliant; it's hard to say "this isn't your best work – you can do better. You need to work on X." On the other hand, I have a musician friend who is a great musician but we have very different perspectives. When we don't agree on things I know I'm on the right track. He always gives me negative feedback on my best work. You have to know where people are coming from.

Feedback is more likely to be perceived as accurate when provided by a credible source. And when feedback is seen as accurate, it's more likely to be accepted and used. Recipients will perceive feedback as fair, and be more motivated to use it, when it comes from a source with whom they have a positive relationship (Pat-El, Tillema, & van Koppen, 2012; Sparr & Sonnentag, 2008). People also tend to be more motivated to use feedback when they believe that the provider is competent in whatever domain is being discussed (Steelman, Levy, & Snell, 2004). Feedback does not occur in a vacuum. It's not simply a transaction (although some people treat it as such). It's a human interaction steeped in the emotions, history, and expectations we have of one another. Not only does the existing relationship between the feedback provider and feedback recipient affect the dynamics and impact of a feedback discussion, that feedback discussion also contributes to and shapes the future of the relationship. Feedback provided constructively and with care can help to build trust and enhance the relationship over time, whereas destructive or unhelpful feedback provided without thought and care can quickly erode a relationship.

Message. What the feedback source says and how they choose to frame it impacts what we hear, how we react to it, and what we choose to do with it. Feedback can be either positive or negative. Positive feedback tells us that performance is on track to meet our goals, or that we have already met or exceeded our goals or expectations. Negative feedback highlights a gap between our current state and our goals or expectations. Negative feedback gets a bad rap. People often incorrectly use "negative" to mean bad, unconstructive, or poorly delivered feedback. Taking a control theory perspective, "negative" simply means that current behavior has not yet met goals or expectations and that there is a deficit to close. The magic of negative feedback is that it can tell us what needs to happen to close that gap and to, ultimately, achieve our goals. Although negative feedback can actually have more utility, people tend to react more favorably to positive feedback (Anseel & Lievens, 2006). Positive feedback elicits positive emotions, tells them that their efforts have paid off, and indicates that no additional work is needed to achieve a goal.

Feedback can focus on how you're doing on something you're currently working on (*process feedback*), or provide an overall evaluation of how you did, once something has been completed (*outcome feedback*). Process feedback is more conducive to behavior change and immediate course correction, whereas outcome feedback feels like a final evaluation. As we'll see in Chapter 2, these two types have a significant impact on how we react to feedback – particularly when we cross these types with feedback sign (positive versus negative). Feedback is also more likely to be accepted and viewed favorably when it is relevant to the recipient's goals or whatever task they are currently focused on (Jawahar, 2010; Steelman et al., 2004).

The way that a feedback provider chooses to frame feedback impacts its effectiveness. Feedback can either focus on a *person* or on their *behavior*. Person-focused feedback refers to who someone is as a person – their capabilities, personality, or character – whereas behavior-focused feedback refers to their observable actions or behaviors. Not surprisingly, people are more likely to get defensive and reject negative feedback that focuses on them as a person, as opposed to their behavior. Negative person-focused feedback can feel like a character attack. Not only is it less likely to be accepted, it's also *harder* to use! Changing your behavior is much easier than changing who you are as a person. Feedback that focuses on actions or behaviors is more likely to be accepted and is also more conducive to future behavior change. Surprisingly, providing positive feedback on someone's abilities can make them less resilient to future challenges because they attribute their success to their abilities, rather than their hard work or effort (Dweck, 2006).

The lens that a feedback provider applies to their message impacts the likelihood that feedback will be accepted and used. The great irony of feedback is that it is entirely backward-looking, yet we give it to influence future behavior. It's not uncommon for a feedback recipient to get defensive or feel unmotivated to act in response to feedback on past events. The event has come and gone, and it's too late to do anything about it. Recent research has shown that making feedback forward-looking can bridge the gap between events that occurred in the past and doing something different in the future (Roberts, Levy, Dahling, Riordan, & O'Malley, 2019). Forward-looking feedback (FLF) uses past events as data points but quickly flips the focus of the conversation toward "next time" or "if this were to happen again in the future." Our understanding of the impact of FLF is still limited, but feedback providers can use this technique to avoid a debate about the past and instead focus on opportunities for the future.

Context. Where, when, and how feedback is provided – the context – influences how feedback is perceived and received. In general, feedback should be provided as soon as possible after an event occurs, while the event is still fresh in the minds of the giver and the recipient (Hays, Kornell, & Bjork, 2013; van der Kleij, Eggen, Timmers, & Veldkamp, 2012). If the purpose of feedback is to help people to adjust their behavior to be more effective, timely feedback enables more real-time behavior change and is more likely to result in improved performance. One exception to the "as soon as possible" rule is to wait until feedback can be provided in a private setting (Ashford & Northcraft, 1992). Receiving feedback in public can be uncomfortable and activate self-consciousness in the recipient that takes their attention away from improving their behavior, and instead focuses their attention inward to their own discomfort and insecurities.

Feedback providers also have a choice in when and how to provide feedback, and must consider what medium will be the most effective given the situation. Today, compared to 20 years ago, we have a multitude of choices in how and when to provide feedback. Research has consistently shown that a face-to-face discussion is the preferred delivery method for most people (Au & Chan, 2013), but in many modern workplaces, an in-person feedback conversation is not always possible. There are advantages and disadvantages of using other media, like videoconferencing or phone, written feedback (e.g., in an email or comments in a document), or text or chat. Interestingly, feedback provided face-to-face (which could be in person or via live video) is the most likely to be inflated. When a feedback provider has to look their recipient in the eye, delivering tough messages may feel harder, leading them to water down their feedback (Waung & Highhouse, 1997). Every medium has pros and cons, and the key to choosing an effective delivery method is aligning the goals and sensitivity of the topic with the advantages of the delivery method. For example, Frances, an attorney in Paris, "texts [her] clients to give them immediate feedback to change their behavior when a situation is escalating."

Given her goal of alerting the client about their behavior immediately, texting is an appropriate choice. A more extensive discussion of the client's behavior may follow, but texting enables immediate feedback and course correction. A formal performance review, however, does not demand this level of immediacy and is better suited to a planned conversation. Chapter 3 explores the impact of technology in shifting the feedback landscape over the last few decades.

Context also includes the overall environment in which feedback is provided. Intangibles, such as a culture of psychological safety and learning, significantly impact the success of a feedback exchange. Researcher Amy Edmondson (1999) notes that organizations with high levels of psychological safety – where individuals feel comfortable being themselves, taking risks, or making mistakes – better support feedback seeking and learning. When people experience a sense of psychological safety they are less likely to worry about being judged, embarrassed, or punished for their behavior. As a result, they are more likely to set challenging goals, speak up, ask for help, and take risks (Li & Tan, 2013). Similarly, learning cultures promote growth, development, self-awareness, and improved performance by empowering individuals to feel supported in taking risks, making mistakes, and giving, receiving, and asking for feedback. Learning cultures promote "inquiry and dialogue" (Yang, Watkins, & Marsick, 2004) and encourage people to ask for feedback and experiment with behaviors (London, 2003), whereas performance cultures focus disproportionately on demonstrating and proving competence.

Every organization has a *feedback environment* that influences norms and behaviors related to giving, accepting, and using feedback (London & Smither, 2002; Steelman et al., 2004). The feedback environment is part of the intangible culture that is created and constantly evolving as a result of leader and employee behaviors. An organization's feedback environment is shaped both from the top down (leaders impacting the rest of the organization) and from the bottom up (employees' day-to-day feedback behavior shaping the overall culture). In a positive or robust feedback environment colleagues regularly give, ask for, and apply feedback. They see feedback as a way to grow and improve performance, and to communicate effectively with their colleagues. On the other hand, employees in organizations with weak or negative feedback environments hesitate to seek out or offer feedback. Asking for or receiving feedback may be perceived as a sign of weakness, self-doubt, or low performance. The feedback environment where someone works shapes (and can be shaped by) their personal attitudes toward feedback. Working in an organization with a strong, positive feedback environment can help individuals strengthen and develop their own feedback orientation. Since a feedback environment can develop from the bottom up, an employee base with strong feedback orientations can drive a stronger feedback environment over time.

Recipient. An individual's feedback orientation is one of several attributes that impact how they perceive and engage with feedback. People are complex, multifaceted, and shaped by years of past experiences. It's no wonder, then, that preferences, personality, and tendencies influence how people respond to feedback. When an individual has a strong feedback orientation, they value, use, and seek out feedback (Linderbaum & Levy, 2010). On the other hand, having a weak feedback orientation can translate to avoiding, disliking, and disregarding others' feedback. A person's feedback orientation develops through years and years of feedback interactions. Fortunately, it is a dynamic attitude that can become more robust when someone works in a positive feedback environment, and learns or chooses to like, value, use, and proactively seek out feedback.

Developing a sense of self-efficacy – both general self-efficacy and related to handling feedback – can help people become more resilient to, see the value in, and use negative feedback. When someone has high self-efficacy, it means they believe that they are capable of achieving their goals or completing whatever task is in front of them (Bandura, 1986). Self-efficacy is different from self-confidence. It can apply to specific tasks or situations (as opposed to a global sense of self) and is developed over time by demonstrating to ourselves what we are capable of. Feedback plays an important role in helping people understand how they are performing against goals and expectations. As a result, encouraging feedback that helps us to see the impact of our efforts actually builds self-efficacy over time. Similarly, low self-efficacy and low self-esteem can drive people to react defensively in response to negative feedback, to reject or actively avoid feedback, and to opt not to use it. People who are high in self-efficacy are more likely to value, use, and seek out feedback (Brown, Ganesan, & Challagalla, 2001; Heslin, Latham, & VandeWalle, 2005).

Other personal attitudes and attributes affect our feedback behavior, such as whether we are more focused on learning (learning oriented) or demonstrating our competence (performance oriented). Just as organizations can be more oriented toward learning or performance, so, too, can individuals. People who are learning and growth oriented value feedback as a way to become more self-aware, to learn from their actions and behaviors, and to identify opportunities to be more effective in the future. On the other hand, people who are performance oriented are motivated to demonstrate their competence. Negative feedback is a threat to this goal, as opposed to a valuable source of information. Similarly, people high in trait anxiety or neuroticism (one of the Big Five personality traits) are less likely to accept, use, and ask for feedback, whereas people high in the Big Five personality dimension of conscientiousness tend to be more motivated to use feedback and also to have higher performance after putting their feedback to use (Colquitt, LePine, & Noe, 2000; Dominick, Reilly, & Byrne, 2004).

Our Big Five personality traits tend to be stable across our lifetime, but other attitudes, like self-efficacy, learning orientation, and feedback orientation can be cultivated and developed. Our feedback behavior is influenced by these attitudes and attributes, and feedback can also help to *strengthen* those attitudes and attributes. High self-efficacy leads us to value feedback, and constructive feedback can further strengthen our self-efficacy. People can make an intentional choice to strengthen their feedback orientation and related attitudes, putting them on a path to being more learning and growth oriented and more self-aware. But, in order to get there, they have to realize that they have the choice, and be willing to embrace the temporary discomfort of accepting and asking for feedback more regularly.

Applying This Model

Think about a few recent feedback experiences that you've had. Can you map those experiences to this four-part model of feedback? If the feedback exchange didn't go particularly well, where did the breakdown occur? In instances where you received feedback, did the problem stem from the feedback source – who gave you the feedback, your relationship with them, your perceptions of them, their behavior? Was it what they said (message) or when, where, or how they provided it (context)? As feedback recipient, what role did you play in the success or failure of the feedback exchange? Did you take ownership for your experience? Did your own feedback orientation or self-esteem derail your reaction to the feedback?

This four-part model is valuable because it helps us to break down and think through any feedback exchange, no matter how difficult or mundane it may be. Feedback feels less intimidating when we parse it out into component parts and use a structure to think through exactly what we want to say, when, where, and how we want to say it. This model also drives home the point that both the feedback provider and the recipient play important roles in the discussion. Although, as a feedback recipient, it is easy to feel like feedback is "happening to" you, the reality is you are an equal participant in the interaction.

For example, Christopher, an alumni team member of Back on My Feet,[3] has learned over time how to respond to feedback constructively. He notes that it's a constant effort, that he:

> used to be more reactive. I would push away and bury problems and conflict, not face them. They would escalate. I still have those emotional reactions, that feeling like I'm being judged. But now I know how to recognize my reaction and pause. I say to myself, "I feel like I'm being judged. Am I being judged? What is this person's perspective?" Then I'll ask them questions to better understand where they are coming from.

Once a feedback provider offers their observations, the recipient has a choice about how they want to respond. We can see the exchange as a one-way transaction – simply accepting what the other person has said and either taking it at face value or being ruled by an immediate emotional reaction. Or, like Christopher, we can pause, recognize our reaction, and take ownership for our experience. You can look at feedback like a cannonball fired by the other person, or see it as a tennis match – you served up this feedback, and now I will hit the ball back over the net with a constructive response, such as asking clarifying questions, sharing my own perspective on the situation, or asking for guidance on what would be more effective.

What's Holding You Back?

What could be possible if you gave all of that (constructive and well-intended!) feedback you've been holding inside for so long? For the coworker who doesn't realize his phone voice is basically a shout? For your spouse who you wish would finish that project started long ago? For your friend who doesn't realize what dating mistakes she's making? And what if they told you all the things that they've been holding inside? How your hair would look so much better in a new style? That you say "you know" a lot when you make presentations? Or that you have spinach in your teeth? When well-intended, useful feedback flows freely everyone has a clearer understanding of how they are impacting and impacted by the world around them.

Feedback given the right way doesn't feel jarring or painful and can truly help people have increased self-awareness and grow and develop. Decades of research on feedback have uncovered the critical nuances that make feedback most effective and easy to receive, but that research rarely makes it from academic journals to everyday life. The purpose of this book is to highlight those feedback best practices and present them in a way that makes them easy to understand and apply right away. In the chapters that follow we will dive deep into the nuances and challenges of giving effective feedback, including specific guidance for being more effective at giving, receiving, asking for, and using feedback.

Try It

Pick a day and log all of your feedback experiences. Note every time you give, receive, ask for, or use feedback. What do you notice? How many of those experiences are "formal" feedback exchanges versus relatively mundane ones? What surprises you about your day of feedback?

Looking for More?

The four-part feedback model introduced in this chapter originated in Gregory and Levy's *Using Feedback in Organizational Consulting* (2015). Those authors reviewed several classic feedback models and distilled the core concepts of each into these four elements: The source, the message, the context, and the recipient. Check out their book to learn more about the classic research that informed this simple four-part model, or to learn more about the nuances of each element.

Notes

1 Pavlov was a behavioral psychologist who found that, after consistently pairing their dinner with the ringing of a bell, dogs would eventually begin to salivate at the sound of the bell, even when no food was presented. In this context, I'm suggesting that people learn to have a strong negative reaction to the word "feedback," even when they don't know for sure that the feedback will be negative or critical.
2 Reprinted with permission from APA.
3 Back on My Feet is a nonprofit operating in 13 US cities that helps individuals experiencing homelessness reinvent their lives through running. Members go through extraordinary personal transformation and, ultimately, land in independent housing, with full-time employment.

CHAPTER 2

WHAT GETS IN THE WAY

When someone waits a while to give me feedback, I feel like it could have helped me but I get it too late. When my teacher says, "you could have done X" or "you should have learned this last year" it feels unfair and frustrating. It's totally backward looking.

Justice, 14 years old

Someone asked me, "Why do you find feedback so interesting?" I paused and thought to myself,

What about feedback is NOT interesting? It's a valuable source of information, it tells you what you're doing right, it tells you what you need to do to improve, it helps you achieve your goals … why is this even a question?

In that moment I had an epiphany – what I find so interesting about feedback is that *it tells you about yourself relative to the world around you*. Without feedback, we would operate in a vacuum.

In a scene in the film *The Aviator*, filmmaker Howard Hughes (played by Leonardo DiCaprio) forces a reshoot of a wild flight sequence because the sky is too clear. There were no clouds, no buildings, just planes and blue sky – no reference points. As a result, the viewer would be unable to fully discern how fast the planes were flying, or how wild and risky their flight moves were. Reshot with clouds in the sky, the scene was suddenly more exciting and suspenseful. The clouds provided reference points that enabled the viewer to understand the real impact and detail of the aviators' actions.

Think of feedback as the distance between those planes and the clouds. It helps us to understand how others see us, where we stand with respect to our goals, successes, and failures, and reflects information back to us about ourselves in the world.

But, as we saw in Chapter 1, many people miss out on this valuable data because they dislike and actively avoid receiving or asking for feedback. From the moment they enter the world, children are surrounded by feedback, which shapes their understanding of themselves and the world around them. In a short time children develop attitudes and beliefs about feedback. A study of children and adolescent feedback-seeking behavior found that children as young as 11 actively seek out feedback to verify their self-perceptions (Cassidy, Ziv, Mehta, & Feeney, 2003). Not unlike many other aspects of childhood, those beliefs and perceptions are quickly influenced by the behavior of others around us. Experiences over time, starting in childhood, shape the negative connotation of and negative emotions that many people have toward feedback, which can lead them to have a hardwired emotional reaction to feedback. The culmination of feedback experiences with parents, teachers, coaches, camp counselors, and, later, professors, bosses, colleagues, and partners shapes our overall attitude toward feedback: Our feedback orientation. Chances are, most of these influential individuals in our lives are not well versed in feedback best practices.

Feedback Providers Behaving Badly

Negative experiences with feedback, which shape our ongoing feedback beliefs and attitudes, are largely attributable to the behaviors and choices of feedback providers – what they say (the message), and how, when, and where they choose to say it (context). It's easy to forget that, as a feedback recipient, we are 50% of the feedback exchange, when so much of that feedback exchange is disproportionately impacted by the feedback provider. Whether or not they realize it, feedback providers have a wide range of choices in how they give feedback to others: Their actual words and what they focus on, how long they wait to deliver it, when and where they provide it, and the way they frame and communicate the message.

When, Where, and How: Choosing the Context

The choices that feedback providers make about when and how to provide feedback can unintentionally set up a feedback exchange for disaster. Most people deeply dislike receiving feedback in public – particularly negative feedback (Ashford & Northcraft, 1992; Levy, Albright, Cawley, & Williams, 1995). Perhaps the only thing worse than feeling criticized is being criticized in front of your peers, colleagues, classmates, or even random strangers. I once had the troubling experience of hearing a manager loudly provide detailed negative feedback to one of her team members in the middle of an office kitchen during lunch, for all to hear. The team member looked mortified, as if he wanted to run away (later in this chapter we'll talk about the role of the amygdala in feedback exchanges – this is where your fight, flight, or freeze impulse originates). I'm willing to bet he was so focused on his own discomfort that he didn't absorb much of the feedback. Public criticism likely activated his sense of self-consciousness, which draws attention inward to the self, and away from hearing the actual feedback.

As a rule of thumb, negative feedback is best given in private, but time is also of the essence. Waiting too long to provide negative feedback can evoke feelings of frustration, anger, and apathy, and reduce the likelihood that people will accurately remember what happened in the first place. When feedback is timely – following closely on the heels of the behavior or situation – people are more likely to pay attention and also retain the feedback (van der Kleij, Eggen, Timmers, & Veldkamp, 2012). "Why did you wait so long to tell me this?" is an understandable reaction to long-delayed negative feedback, and would likely be accompanied by little interest in the actual feedback. Long delays can send a message that the feedback provider doesn't really care or that it wasn't a priority. Additionally, the window to take action and address the issue or behavior may have passed.

As mentioned in Chapter 1, feedback providers have many choices as to how they will deliver feedback. Today alone, I have received feedback from other people via text, email, Slack, Instagram, by phone, and in person. Technology is wonderful because it enables us to provide timely, specific process feedback – such as comments on a document, a quick note about a project via instant message or text, and suggestions for tomorrow's meeting based on a meeting today. However, when used inappropriately these tools also create a lot of urgency and ambiguity. The problem with texts, emails, and instant messages is that you don't always know what the person on the other end is working on.

Receiving negative feedback via email or text message when you are in the middle of something and not expecting it can be a deeply distracting and off-putting experience. Not only does it disrupt whatever you are currently working on, it also diminishes the impact of the feedback, as you will be more likely to disregard it, have a negative reaction to it, or dismiss it altogether. Inferring emotional tone in a text or email is also common – leading even the most balanced person to misinterpret the meaning and intent of an otherwise innocuous message.

In addition to how they frame the feedback, when and where they provide the feedback, and what medium they choose, the actual feedback provider themselves can be part of the problem. As mentioned in Chapter 1, in order for a feedback recipient to be open and accepting of feedback, they must first perceive the feedback provider as trustworthy and credible (Ilgen, Fisher, & Taylor, 1979). Feedback from an untrustworthy source is likely to be diminished or disregarded, as is feedback provided by an individual who we consider unknowledgeable about the topic or situation. Feedback from people we do not trust or perceive as credible may elicit feelings of doubt (*This guy has no idea what he's talking about*), irritation or anger (*Who does she think she is, telling me this – she's completely incompetent!*), or fear (*Are they lying? Are they trying to set me up for failure?*).

For example, Finch, a wealth advisor, knows that without an established relationship, trust, or credibility, her feedback and advice fall on deaf ears. Says Finch,

> I am an advisor – what I offer to clients is advice. That is my product. And all advice is essentially feedback, so feedback is also my product and plays a very pivotal role in everything I do. I have to find ways to make it effective. I can give people statistics, data, etc. but if the relationship isn't in a healthy place the advice won't be productive or effective – clients either won't hear it or will not apply it. And your feedback and advice is your value. So if the client doesn't hear it or accept it, you lose your value. In order for my feedback to be heard I have to build the relationship so they know that I care, to get to that place so I can actually offer feedback and advice from a place of trust and credibility. Ultimately I can't give the best investment management advice without knowing and understanding the person – their goals, aspirations, their financial health, etc.

Trust and credibility are foundational for a feedback exchange to be effective. It's easy to see a feedback conversation as a transaction or an exchange of information but, ultimately, it's a very human interaction, steeped in emotion, past experiences together, and assumptions and judgments of one another.

Feedback Type

Unsurprisingly, people tend to have the strongest emotional reaction in response to negative feedback (Ilies, De Pater, & Judge, 2007). As mentioned in Chapter 1, negative feedback simply means feedback that highlights a gap or deficit between our current state and our desired or goal state. Negative feedback is often misconstrued as "poorly delivered feedback" or "overtly, painfully critical feedback." A softer term used in many organizations as an alternative to "negative feedback" is "constructive feedback." But, let's be real here – shouldn't ALL feedback be constructive? Positive or negative – why would you want to give feedback that is not constructive, unless you are a Mean Girl or deliberately trying to make someone feel cut down. As a feedback purist, I'm going to stick with "negative feedback" for the duration of this book because "negative feedback" is not a dirty word (and by the end of this book I hope you feel the same way).

Because negative feedback highlights a deficit between the current state and the goal or desired state, it can elicit negative emotions – like disappointment, anxiety, frustration, fear, or demotivation. For example, say you own a restaurant and are hoping for two Michelin Stars this year (your goal). Learning that you have been awarded only one Michelin Star – despite being a huge honor – is technically negative feedback because you fell short of reaching your goal of two stars. Whereas many chefs or restauranteurs would be thrilled with the news of receiving a Michelin Star, in this instance you may experience anger, frustration, disappointment, or sadness because you still have a gap between your current state (one star) and your desired state (two stars).

This example highlights the importance of feedback *type*, and its interaction with feedback sign (positive versus negative). Learning about your Michelin Star award for the year is an example of *outcome* feedback – a final, overall assessment of your performance. Other examples of outcome feedback include an annual performance rating, a final grade in a class, news about whether or not you were selected for a job, whether you receive the gold medal or the silver medal in the 100 meter dash. Contrast this with *process* feedback, which tells you how you are doing along the way, as you are working on something, before you reach the final outcome.

Process feedback is much more conducive to helping people adjust their behavior in order to achieve their goals. Process feedback is given "along the way" and therefore lends itself to being incorporated into our work and efforts. Specific process feedback enables feedback recipients to act with agility and course correct their behavior before it's too late. On the other hand, receiving only outcome feedback can be unhelpful and demoralizing. If we don't know how we are doing along the way (e.g., if we don't receive process feedback), and then find out at the end of our efforts that we have missed our target, a sense of failure and demotivation is common. At this point, it's too late to do something with the feedback, and all we know is that we didn't achieve what we'd been striving for, despite our best efforts.

In school, feedback from your professor and grades on assignments are all considered process feedback leading up to your final grade. At work, process feedback includes day-to-day feedback from your manager, customers, clients, or colleagues. Many organizations have adopted performance management processes that encourage quarterly check-ins or conversations between managers and employees. These check-ins are examples of process feedback and are typically non-evaluative. A hallmark of outcome feedback, on the other hand, is that it *is* evaluative.

Crossing feedback type (outcome versus process) with feedback sign (positive versus negative), results in four distinct combinations, which, in turn, evoke very different responses from recipients (Medvedeff, Gregory, & Levy, 2008). Not surprisingly, people like positive outcome feedback the most – it lets them know that they have succeeded and did a good job at whatever they were working on. What may surprise you is that the next most popular type of feedback – which leads people to actually ask for *more* subsequent feedback – is negative process feedback. Negative process feedback is "feedback along the way" that tells you where you are off – what you need to do more of, less of, or differently in order to achieve your goals. Herein lies one of my favorite findings of all time about feedback. People don't hate negative feedback – they just hate negative *outcome* feedback, which essentially tells them that they failed at whatever they were doing.

For example, Alex, who is the general manager of a Michelin-starred restaurant, gets frustrated when guests only provide negative outcome feedback.

> When guests tell us at the end of the night – or even later after they have left the restaurant – that they had a bad experience or didn't like something, there is no opportunity to repair the situation. We have set up so many opportunities – in fact, 10 specific opportunities – throughout the meal for guests to provide feedback.

Alex's frustration is understandable. The ten opportunities she and her team have created for guests to provide feedback on their dining experience is classic

FEEDBACK TYPE	FEEDBACK SIGN	
	POSITIVE	NEGATIVE
PROCESS	FEELS GOOD; LIMITED VALUE, TELLS PEOPLE THEY ARE ON THE RIGHT TRACK TO MEET THEIR GOALS. TOO MUCH CAN RESULT IN SLOWING DOWN THEIR EFFORTS OVER TIME (COASTING).	GREATEST INFORMATIONAL VALUE! TELLS SOMEONE THEY ARE OFF ON THEIR GOALS, AND ALSO HOW TO GET BACK ON TRACK.
OUTCOME	FEELS GREAT! TELLS SOMEONE THEY MET THEIR GOAL OR HAD HIGH PERFORMANCE AT THE CONCLUSION OF A TASK, AND NOW THEY'RE DONE.	DEMOTIVATING. TELLS SOMEONE THEY DIDN'T MEET THEIR GOAL OR DELIVER HIGH PERFORMANCE AND THE TASK IS NOW COMPLETE. TOO LATE TO MAKE CHANGES.

Figure 2.1 Crossing feedback sign with feedback type results in four very different types of feedback, some more effective for influencing behavior than others.

process feedback. If guests are unhappy with some aspect of their experience, letting the staff know in the moment enables them to course correct and fix the situation to delight the customers, and achieve their shared goal of having a wonderful dining experience. Sharing only negative outcome feedback is fruitless, because the experience has ended and it's too late for the staff to take action.

Outcome feedback provides an overall evaluation once a project or experience has ended. Negative outcome feedback is likely to result in negative emotional reactions and a drop in motivation. Positive outcome feedback, however, leaves people feeling satisfied and justified in their efforts – their work paid off. In an ideal world, we would all receive specific, negative process feedback that is easy to apply and use and, ultimately, results in positive outcome feedback when we meet our goal. But that's not always realistic, and negative outcome feedback is bound to occur at some point in everyone's life. One adaptive way to reframe uninspiring negative outcome feedback is to expand our time horizon and context, and view outcome feedback as a form of process feedback. For example, if you received a poor annual performance review you can see that review as the ultimate outcome evaluation – I failed. Alternatively, you can look at the 30-year trajectory of your career and see this annual review as one milestone along the way. Interpreting that negative review as feedback to help you have a better year next year is actually a way to reframe outcome feedback into a form of process feedback.

For example, Goodloe, a professional artist, sees feedback that he gets on any particular piece of work as input to his ongoing approach to creating.

> Getting good feedback can be stifling if it makes you complacent and stop striving to change or evolve what you are doing. Negative feedback, even if it makes you doubt what you are doing, there's no way you can say it's a bad thing. Knowing whatever I am doing is not over allows me to incorporate feedback into whatever I will do next. Having that perspective in the back of my mind allows me to incorporate any feedback that I get into my work.

People want, value, and appreciate negative process feedback because it provides a road map for how they need to change their behavior to improve.[1] Process feedback is valuable because it can be put into practice right away, as people are still working on their project or task, and help them to move closer to their goal.

Person versus Behavior-Focused Feedback

There is a caveat to the value of negative process feedback, however. Because it is negative, this feedback can still elicit negative emotions, and must be given with care, even though it is not evaluative. Subtle nuances in the focus of the feedback can make or break its impact. Specifically, **negative feedback that focuses on the *person*, rather than that person's *behavior* is significantly more likely to elicit a defensive reaction.** For example, saying "Noor, you are not a good public speaker" is much more likely to make Noor defensive than, "Noor, your speech today lacked structure and your voice was too quiet so it was hard to follow." The first example focuses on Noor as a person, whereas the second example focuses on Noor's actions – her observable behavior. Receiving feedback that focuses on you as a person feels much more critical, sometimes like a character attack. It provokes feelings of self-consciousness and draws attention inward, away from the task at hand. Person-focused feedback also feels more like an opinion, less evidence based. Not only is person-focused feedback hard to accept, it's also not very helpful. Changing behavior is challenging, but it's *much* easier than attempting to change who you are as a person! In the example, the person-focused feedback is more general and gives Noor no direction on what about her speech was ineffective. The behavior-focused example will enable Noor to do better next time – to give her speech more structure and to speak up.

It's easy to assume that person-focused feedback is only counterproductive for negative feedback. Praising someone for who they are as a person feels generous; we want them to know how great they are as a person. Though it may seem counterintuitive, Carol Dweck's (2006) groundbreaking research found that person-focused (as opposed to behavior-focused) praise can render people less resilient to future failures. For example, if a child gets an "A" on a test, it's tempting to say "Quentin, you got an A on your test! You are so smart!" After repeated instances of Quentin hearing how smart he is after he gets good grades, he learns to associate his success with his abilities. So, one day, when Quentin fails an exam in college, he starts to believe he's not smart, that he doesn't have what it takes to succeed. Just as he always attributed his successes to his abilities, now he's attributing his *lack* of success to his *lack* of ability. Instead, if Quentin had repeatedly been praised for his hard work and preparation, he would have learned to attribute his success to his efforts, rather than his abilities. Therefore, when he fails a test as a college freshman, he will attribute his failure to his missing class and his insufficient studying and preparation, rather than his lack of intelligence. Behavior-focused feedback – both positive and negative – empowers people to see a connection between their efforts and important outcomes, enabling a growth mindset, a stronger sense of self-efficacy, and a belief that they can change their behavior to attain the outcomes that they want. Person-focused feedback, however, conditions people to believe that their abilities determine their successes and failures, and that those abilities are fixed. People with a fixed mindset believe that whether they fail or succeed, it's because of who they are and the hand they have been dealt (Dweck, 2006).

Giving person-focused feedback is a poor choice for both short- and long-term impact. In the short term, person-focused feedback makes people defensive, less likely to accept the feedback, and less likely to actually do something with the feedback. In the long term, it can cultivate a maladaptive fixed mindset that holds people back from changing their behaviors or increasing their efforts to achieve desired outcomes.

Meanwhile, in Your Brain…

These bad feedback practices elicit negative emotions and can lead to feedback being disregarded. But what's really going on beneath the surface? A lifetime of poorly delivered, thoughtless feedback, provided in the wrong place at the wrong time by people who are uncomfortable providing feedback slowly contributes to a hardwired propensity to bristle at the mere mention of the word "feedback." Recent research has shown that this sense of dread isn't just in our minds – it's also in our bodies. And it's not unique to being on the receiving end of feedback – *providing* feedback makes people just as anxious and uncomfortable. When asked to participate in a feedback exchange following a negotiation, both the recipient and the provider showed an increased heart rate (as much as a 50% increase) and higher levels of anxiety (West, Thorson, Grant, & Rock, 2018).

Uncomfortable feedback exchanges evoke the same biological response as a real, tangible threat – such as encountering a lion in the Serengeti or a group of questionable people in a dark alley. The amygdala – the small, almond-shaped emotional center of our brains – is actively engaged in these real and hypothetical threats, and, when activated, prompts us to fight, flee, or freeze. Because our brains are quick, efficient, and lazy processors of information, we learn to anticipate this type of response at the mere mention of the word "feedback."

To ensure our survival in the face of the lion or the questionable people in an alley, our emotional responses to threats are imperceptibly fast. Feedback elicits this same threat response, and therefore a strong, immediate emotional reaction, which instantly interferes with our ability to mindfully process the feedback. The ability to mindfully process feedback – to think about it clearly and rationally – is a precursor to accepting and using that feedback (London & Smither, 2002). Emotions are fast and strong, and can stifle the mindful processing of feedback. In the face of feedback that feels critical, inaccurate, or personal, this instant emotional reaction will lead to feelings of defensiveness and rejection of the feedback before the recipient has even had time to stop and think about it. Feedback exchanges can truly go haywire at this point – turning into a cascade of emotionally charged, fear-based responses from feedback recipient and feedback provider. Failing to give the feedback recipient time and space to process the feedback is another major fail point for feedback providers. "Cool cognition" needs time to catch up with "hot emotion" (this is why we count to ten when we are angry – to give rational thought some time to catch up), and when the feedback recipient does not have time to step back, let the initial emotional reaction pass, and actually process the feedback, the message often gets lost.

The feedback recipient plays an important role in this process – they are not simply a victim or passive recipient of poorly delivered feedback, although they may feel like feedback is "happening to them." A feedback recipient has control over their ability to create time and space to absorb and think about the feedback. They may not be able to control the quality of feedback or feedback delivery, but they *can* control what they do with it – how they react to it, if they ask questions to clarify it, or if they take control of their experience by saying

"I need some time to think about this – let me get back to you later today." The individual differences of the feedback recipient play an important part in the feedback exchange. As mentioned in Chapter 1, we all have a *feedback orientation* – which encapsulates the extent to which we value, use, and proactively seek out feedback (Linderbaum & Levy, 2010). Our feedback orientation is shaped over time by our experiences with feedback – the interactions we have with teachers, coaches, bosses, parents, colleagues – and also the feedback cultures where we live and work. Someone with a strong feedback orientation will be more resilient to and take more ownership of a mediocre feedback experience, as will an individual with high self-esteem or self-confidence (McCauley, Lombardo, & Usher, 1989; Northcraft & Ashford, 1990). Individuals with a weak feedback orientation or low self-esteem or self-confidence are likely to be less resilient and more adversely affected by a low-quality feedback experience. Ironically, these poor experiences further reinforce their weak feedback orientation, contributing to a sort of downward spiral in their ability to handle feedback.

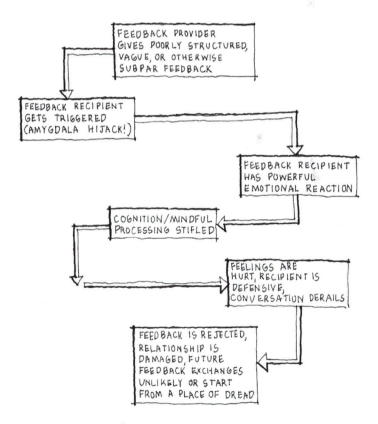

Figure 2.2 A feedback downward spiral (not exactly scientific but also not exactly unscientific).

The common spiral of bad feedback works like this: A feedback provider is uncomfortable giving feedback, doesn't know how to provide effective feedback, doesn't know what he or she is talking about, or has failed to build trust with the feedback recipient. A poor-quality feedback exchange follows, which triggers a powerful, biologically based emotional reaction in the recipient, who then either gets defensive, angry, or withdraws, thus bypassing a moment to pause and really think about the feedback. The feedback (which, all along, could have been extremely helpful, if not so poorly handled) gets lost, ignored, or misinterpreted. The relationship may be damaged, the individual's feedback orientation may be further bruised, and the entire opportunity to help someone learn, develop, or improve their performance has been lost.

Now that we are sufficiently depressed about feedback, let's restore hope in what's possible by exploring four tools that can lead to feedback exchanges that are thoughtful, effective, and strengthen relationships, drive higher performance, and support growth and development.

If You Forget Everything Else from This Book, Remember These Four Things

Decades of psychology, business, and education research have uncovered an array of nuances and best practices that make giving, receiving, and using feedback more effective. You may forget everything else that you read in this book, but I encourage you to take away these four strategies that – in my experience – **are the four simplest and most effective things that you can do to make feedback work.** If you're still hungry for more, Chapters 4, 5, and 6 provide a closer look and more tools and best practices for giving, receiving and asking for, and using feedback.

1: Focus on the *behavior*, not the *person*. Have you ever tried to really change who you are as a person? It's hard. Very hard. And takes a long time. On the other hand, changing your behavior (although still challenging) is much easier. The reason we give feedback is because we want people to do more of something, less of something, or something else entirely. When feedback focuses on observable behaviors, it's much easier for the recipient to understand what they are doing and therefore adjust their behavior for next time. For instance, telling a colleague "you are a terrible public speaker" is significantly less likely to help them improve their public speaking skills than saying, "in your presentation this morning I couldn't hear you because you spoke too softly and looked down at your notes the entire time." The behavior-focused feedback (you spoke too softly and looked down the entire time) is much easier to act on next time (talk louder, look up) than "you are a terrible public speaker" (and what am I supposed to do about it???), because it actually highlights specific behaviors that the recipient can work on next time.

As mentioned previously, Carol Dweck's work on mindset suggests that most people approach their lives and the world through one of two lenses: They either believe that their abilities are "set" (a fixed mindset) or that their abilities can be developed (a growth mindset; Dweck, 2006). Focusing your feedback on behavior (e.g., "you *do* this" or "you *did* this" as opposed to "you *are* this") supports others in their pursuit of growth. People exhibit behaviors but they are not defined by their behavior – behavior can be modified and adapted based on what's working, what's not, and changes in the situation. When you provide someone with behavior-focused feedback, they are more likely to recall the situation and adjust their future behavior accordingly. When you provide person-focused feedback (especially negative feedback), they are significantly more likely to have a strong emotional reaction. Your feedback, however well intended, may feel like a personal attack on their personality, abilities, or character. It's easy to assume that this person-versus-behavior distinction only applies to critical feedback, but recall that positive person-focused feedback can be destructive. Carol Dweck's research has also shown that praising children's abilities when they succeed actually reduces their resilience to future failures. Remember, if a child gets an "A" on a test and their parent showers them with praise about how brilliant and clever they are, the child learns to attribute success to their abilities. Later in the school year when that child gets a "C" on a test, they assume that they are stupid because they have learned to equate performance with ability. On the other hand, if you praise a child's effort and hard work, they are more likely to repeat that behavior in the future and attribute their successes and failures to their *behavior*, not their innate abilities.

Focus on *observable* behaviors in your feedback and ideally things that you have seen with your own eyes. Fight the temptation to make inferences about what's happening in someone's head – you can't see their thoughts or their reasoning. Offering your opinion, your subjective interpretation of why they did what they did, or a judgment about their actions is likely to be met with defensiveness and irritation. Your feedback is significantly more likely to be accepted and used if it's evidence based – focused on observable behaviors that you've seen with your own eyes.

Even better is focusing on the specific task or end product. If you are able to direct your feedback to a "thing" that the person was working on, feedback becomes even more objective and less likely to provoke an emotionally charged reaction. For example, say a graphic design colleague developed the visuals for a report you've been working on and you don't love them – it's not quite the look and feel you had in mind. You could focus your feedback on their competence ("I don't think you're able to create what I have in mind"). You could focus on their behavior ("The approach you took in the design isn't really what I had in mind."). Or, you could focus on the actual end product ("The cover design is a little busier than what I had in mind. I would prefer something cleaner and simpler."). Of course not all situations include a tangible end product where you can focus your feedback. When task-based feedback isn't an option, focus on observable behaviors.

2: Be as specific as possible. In the example of the colleague with the lackluster public speaking performance, you may have noticed another nuance: The behavior-focused feedback ("you spoke too softly and looked down at your notes the entire time") is significantly more specific than the person-focused feedback ("you are a terrible public speaker"). Behavior change is hard. And the more general or vague feedback is, the harder it is to act on. The best feedback is as specific as possible. We often think and communicate in generalities, but actually "operate" at a much lower level of abstraction. For instance, if I tell my husband, "we need to paint the house," the process of actually painting the house happens through a series of little behaviors: Decide if we'll paint or hire painters, prioritize which rooms to paint first, choose paint colors, figure out how much paint we need, what our budget is, when we'll get it done, move furniture, etc. Feedback focused on a lower level of abstraction (e.g., zoomed in on specific, isolated behaviors) is easier for the recipient to accept and use (Kluger & DeNisi, 1996).

Humans are natural problem solvers. We don't like it when something is amiss. When we are grumpy or in pain, we search for specific causes so that we can take action to feel better. However, when we are happy and content, we rarely search for the reason why. Humans are hardwired to think in more detail and specificity when we are dealing with negative or unpleasant experiences. Research by Bodenhausen, Kramer, and Susser (1994) found that positive emotions motivate us to engage in relatively shallow information processing, whereas negative emotions indicate to us that some problem needs to be solved so we think and process information at a greater level of depth and detail. The same is true of feedback. We tend to be much more specific when providing negative feedback, and more general with our praise. Think about your own experiences – how often does the positive feedback you receive only go as far as "great job!," "that was awesome!," "amazing," "really nice work," "good playing out there," etc. When was the last time someone actually gave you detailed, behavior-based feedback about things that you are doing well? Although specific negative feedback is the most helpful for achieving goals and improving performance (it tells you exactly what you need to address to perform better), it's also very important to understand specifically what we are doing well.

For example, Parker, a yoga teacher and studio owner, found that the specific feedback she received in her teacher training felt valuable, personalized, and easy to implement.

> My instructors provided feedback that was totally tailored to me. For some of my classmates who were more sensitive the feedback was softer, but mine was very technical. I'm very open to feedback and was eager to learn and improve; they could see my ego would not be bruised. I remember getting feedback on five very specific topics. The feedback was easy to apply immediately – both in those workshops and later when I was leading classes. It was very specific and I really trusted their advice. My instructors knew what they were talking about and I completely saw the value in their feedback and advice.

Back in 2010 I attended a learning session with the Center for Creative Leadership, where I was introduced to the Situation-Behavior-Impact (SBI) framework for giving feedback (Weitzel, 2000). I find this framework useful for two reasons: One, it ensures that feedback is specific and behavior based and, two, it forces the feedback provider to pause and think about what they want to say before they say it. I'm always surprised by how many people just blurt out feedback without taking a few minutes to think about how their message could be interpreted by the other person, or if there is a better way to frame their message. If we revisit our public speaking example, we offer the situation – "in your presentation this morning" – so that the recipient knows exactly when the event occurred. We focus on the behavior – "you spoke too softly and looked down at your notes the entire time" – and state the impact and why it matters – "I couldn't hear you." In this case, our point about impact could be even stronger: "In this morning's presentation, you spoke very softly and looked down at your notes the entire time. As a result, I couldn't hear you and I think some of your important messages were lost on the audience." Focusing on the impact that their behavior had on you (e.g., "I couldn't hear you") makes feedback harder to refute. It's hard for a feedback recipient to get defensive and push back on how you feel, what your experience was, or why something mattered to you. After all, feelings are facts – the way you feel isn't right or wrong, it just *is*.

You can use the SBI framework for any kind of feedback. Think about what you want to say, say it, then stop talking. Many people get uncomfortable giving feedback and keep rambling on. This leads to the message getting lost and the feedback provider often digging themselves into an awkward hole. Use the SBI model to pause and think about what you want to say, say it, and then stop talking.

3: Make your feedback forward-looking. Feedback is by definition backward-looking. We share observations about something that has happened in the past in an attempt to influence future behavior. The problem is, we can't change the past. One reason many people get defensive in the face of traditional feedback is because there is nothing they can do about it. If I give you feedback about yesterday's performance, last week's dinner, this morning's team meeting, what can you do but wait for the next opportunity? By simply changing the lens on feedback to make it forward-looking we can help people to get a "do-over" and offer clear solutions for next time. For example, rather than telling your hairstylist, "I didn't like the layers you put in my hair last month," remedy the situation by adding, "this time I'd prefer fewer layers and a more consistent length all around." Or, to go back to our colleague working on their public speaking, rather than stopping with, "you spoke too softly and looked down at your notes the entire time," continue with "when you present at the town hall next week try speaking up, or ask for a microphone, and see if you can use the teleprompter so you don't have to look down at your notes."

Another approach to forward-looking feedback is to apply a coaching approach to the conversation. One hallmark of effective coaching is the use of open-ended questions to draw out the other person – to help them problem solve, reflect, and have ownership for whatever solution they come up with. Complementing feedback with an open-ended question can help to move people from a defensive mindset to one of creative problem-solving. For example, with our hairstylist example, we could say "I didn't like the layers you put in my hair last month. What can we do differently this time to give my hair more body and texture?" Or, for our public speaker friend, "you spoke too softly and looked down at your notes the entire time. When you speak at next week's town hall what could you do differently so we can make sure people hear your important message?" This simple question offers the recipient a chance at redemption. Sure, last time didn't go so well, but let's learn from it and focus on next time.

4: Provide your feedback as soon as possible. Are you one of the millions of people who has put a greasy pizza box or plastic clamshell in your recycling bin, assuming that you are doing the right thing? Me too. Knowing what to recycle versus trash can feel like a one-way, black hole decision. We put things in the bin, put the bin outside, and later find it empty, just to start all over again. Unfortunately, unrecyclable materials can disrupt the quality and usability of entire loads of recyclable materials. We recyclers could be sabotaging recycling efforts without realizing it, all the while believing that we are doing the right thing. In Washington, DC, however, recycling collectors have implemented a valuable feedback loop. When residents include nonrecyclable items in their bin, they receive a note (and the unrecyclable item back) with feedback on what to exclude from future pickups. The feedback is specific – telling residents exactly what was wrong with their pickup, forward-looking (don't include it next time!), and timely. Feedback is given on unrecyclable items on the day of pickup, so that residents can immediately act on the feedback and exclude the unrecyclable items in the following week's pickup.

Feedback is most effective when provided as soon as possible after the situation occurs – for two reasons. One, the situation and behavior will still be fresh in the minds of both the feedback provider and the recipient, resulting in more accurate feedback and more accurate recall of what happened in the situation. Two, timely feedback shows that the feedback provider cares. A long delay between the focal event and feedback on that event may evoke a "why did you wait so long to tell me this?" reaction, plus frustration and defensiveness from the recipient. Research has shown that the shorter the time interval between the event and the feedback, the more likely recipients are to a) pay attention to the feedback, b) accurately recall what happened in the situation, and c) actually use the feedback to improve their performance next time (Ammons, 1956; Hays, Kornell, & Bjork, 2013; van der Kleij et al., 2012). Timely delivery suggests that the feedback is valuable, the situation important, and the provider well intentioned.

The one caveat to the best practice of being as timely as possible is ensuring that you are in an appropriate setting to provide feedback. For most people, "appropriate" means private. As we saw earlier in this chapter, in general, people are significantly less likely to accept, use, or seek additional feedback when it is given in public, in front of others. Recall the story from earlier in the chapter, where I had the misfortune of overhearing a challenging feedback conversation between a manager and a team member in the middle of the open office kitchen. I was appalled that the manager had decided that the open, public workplace kitchen was an appropriate setting for this discussion, and I was sad and embarrassed for the team member being subjected to this public dialogue. The manager's intentions may have been good – perhaps she was focused on the best practice of giving feedback as soon as possible. But she would have been better off waiting until she and the team member were in a private setting, appropriate for a one-to-one dialogue about the team member's performance needs.

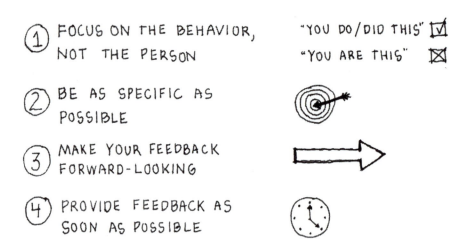

Figure 2.3 If you remember anything, remember these four best practices.

Where the public/private debate gets tricky is in the delivery of praise. Some individuals love being showered with praise in front of other people; for others this experience would be deeply uncomfortable. When it comes to public praise, know your audience. If you have a colleague, friend, family member, etc. who soaks up the spotlight and public adoration – go for it. But, if you're unsure or know your feedback target is more private and eschews the spotlight, wait until you can be in private.

Applying these four practices will render your feedback exchanges materially more effective. I often wonder why people don't give behavior-focused, specific, timely, and forward-looking feedback, but I suspect it's an example of feedback best practices not making it out of scientific journals and into people's living rooms, offices, kitchens, etc. Chapters 4, 5, and 6 include many more suggestions and best practices to try when giving, receiving, asking for, and using feedback. But, before getting to these deep dives, let's take a look at what is new and changing in feedback as a result of technology.

Try It

Notice if you tend to give behavior- or person-focused feedback. If you find that you tend to give feedback to people on their personality, abilities, or character, practice reframing that feedback to focus on observable behavior. If your feedback usually includes "you *are* X," try reframing it to "you *do/did* X."

Looking for More?

Carol Dweck's work on mindsets showed us that some people believe that their abilities are set (fixed mindset), whereas others believe that they have the power and ability to grow, learn, and change (a growth mindset). Learn more in her timeless book, *Mindset: The New Psychology of Success* (2006).

Want to know more about what's happening in your brain when you receive critical feedback? Read *Why Zebras Don't Get Ulcers* by Robert Sapolsky (1994), an enlightening and engaging look at the neurobiology behind our threat response.

Note

1   Positive process feedback has a moderate effect on behavior. It tells you "you're doing fine, keep going." This serves a reinforcing effect, but after enough repeated positive process feedback, participants in this particular study stopped proactively asking for more feedback.

CHAPTER 3

HOW TECHNOLOGY IS CHANGING FEEDBACK

In our business we keep talking about how the world around us is rich with feedback from sources like Yelp and social media. But internally we aren't very good about openly exchanging feedback. It feels like these two worlds are starting to collide.

Adam, Global Leader of Learning and Talent for a multinational real estate firm

Yesterday, I received an email from an online clothing store where I had recently purchased a few items. The email caught my eye because of an "invitation to provide feedback on your purchase." As you can imagine, I perk up anytime I see the word "feedback," and immediately clicked on the email. I expected to find a short online survey where I would provide input on the quality of the products I had purchased, or perhaps on the shopping experience. Instead, I found that the link took me to an online review platform, where I was asked to write an open-ended review that would be posted very publicly on their website. I paused, to consider how feedback in the digital age has taken on a new form and where consumers are able to provide indirect feedback that can meaningfully influence other consumers' choices, oftentimes without sharing their feedback directly with the business.

Social media, smart phones, and wearable technology have added a layer of complexity and immediacy to how we give, receive, and use feedback. Technology increases the availability of feedback and makes it quicker and easier to connect, but can also threaten that precious time for mindful processing and offer a whole new, very public platform for sharing both direct and indirect feedback.

When it comes to technology, who knows better than teenagers. I asked my nieces Nia and Justice how technology impacts their experiences with feedback. They agreed that their peers "can be much harsher on social media or texting, because they aren't face to face with other people." It's easy to feel a false sense of anonymity or, in some instances – like comment features on apps such as YOLO, YouTube, or news sites – actually keep comments anonymous and unattributed. Justice elaborated that,

> it's easier to say things to people on social media or cell phones because you aren't face to face. You don't worry as much about the other person's reaction because you don't have to keep the conversation going. You can just walk away from it whenever you want, which is also good because you can cool off and come back to things later.

Justice's perspective surprised me, because my assumption about teenagers and social media is that they can't get away, unlike pre-tech days when you could go home from school and avoid bullies or other unsavory classmates.

The girls also shared some benefits of technology-enabled feedback. When they post videos on the social video-sharing site TikTok, comments from friends and viewers provide feedback about what makes for funny and entertaining content. They also shared that their iPhone screen time reports provide useful recurring feedback. "We'll get notifications for the week. Our screen time might be 6% higher than last week, which tells us we spent too much time on our phones and will dial it back." After a week of high screen time, they also proactively check their screen time to see how they are tracking with their goals. When Nia and Justice told me about this, I was excited to tell them what a great example this is of control theory, which yielded some important feedback for me (facial expressions that said, "Aunt Brodie you are a huge nerd").

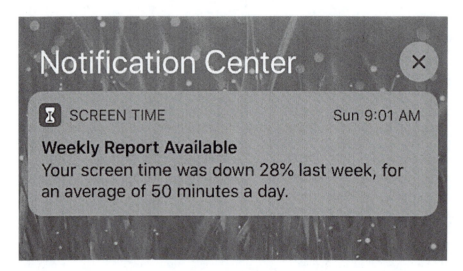

Figure 3.1 Smartphone-generated feedback (such as from the iPhone, shown here) can help users become more aware of how much time they are spending on their phones.

Tech-Enabled Feedback, Person-to-Person

As we saw in Chapter 2, most people still prefer traditional feedback delivered face-to-face (Au & Chan, 2013). But as work environments change and technology further infiltrates our lives, options for providing feedback via some form of technology continue to increase. For individuals who work from home or in virtual roles, every day is filled with technology-enabled interactions such as leveraging tools like email and videoconference, collaboration tools such as Slack, feedback and comments in electronic documents like Microsoft Office or Google Docs, texts, or instant messages, and old-fashioned phone calls (and with mobile phones colleagues can plunge into our days at any time, any place).

For individuals who prefer face-to-face feedback, video calls (e.g., Skype, Zoom, FaceTime) are the best tech-enabled option. Video calls allow the feedback provider and the feedback recipient to see one another's expressions and body language, which are critical inputs for effective dialogue. Video can also reduce the risk of distraction by providing each individual a visual to focus on, and creating a sense of accountability for remaining present and focused on the conversation (it's harder to multitask when you know the other person can see you!). Phone calls also offer the benefit of connecting in real time, sharing feedback in a timely manner, and the ability to hear tone, but they lack the rich visual stimuli of a video call. Tone of voice conveys important information about emotion, but the absence of body language and facial expressions can impede empathy and understanding from being part of the feedback discussion. Although cell phones enable rapid and real-time feedback, they also introduce the inconvenience and discomfort of taking a call at an inappropriate time. For instance, an individual working in a global organization could receive a phone call from a colleague in another time zone early in the morning or late at night, while having dinner with their family, or attending a child's basketball game. When a feedback provider calls unexpectedly, they have no insight into or control over the context of the feedback conversation. The feedback provider and recipient may be in very different settings and very different mindsets, which can lead to an unproductive and potentially harmful conversation.

A friend shared an example with me, where he answered a work call on his mobile phone on a Friday evening while celebrating a family birthday. The caller, his colleague, provided some tough feedback on a client interaction they had had earlier that week. My friend was not in the physical or mental place to have a conversation like this, and as a result became defensive. The poorly timed negative feedback significantly impacted his mood, which had a spillover effect on his family and the rest of the weekend. In hindsight, both my friend and his colleague (the caller) were in the wrong. His colleague was trying to be efficient, and "check a box" by getting the feedback conversation over with. A more effective course of action would have been to put time on the calendar for the following Monday and have the conversation when they were both in the right setting and mindset to have a productive feedback discussion. My friend could also have handled the situation more effectively. He shared that he is prone to the unhealthy belief that "feedback happens to me," rather than seeing himself as a full 50% participant in the feedback conversation. If he could replay this experience all over again, he would have either a) not answered the call or b) told his colleague that now wasn't the right time to have this conversation, let's get time on Monday.

The ever-present and at times intrusive nature of technology requires ownership and self-management to keep the potential flow of feedback manageable and in check. Text, email, instant message, and other collaboration tool alerts have the potential to infiltrate our lives all day, every day, and each one is a quick and easy vehicle for providing feedback. Feedback providers' choice of medium is as equally important as their choice of message when planning to provide feedback. Factors to consider when choosing a medium include the urgency of the message (e.g., your boss is about to meet a client for lunch and has been calling her the wrong name, so you quickly text your boss to remind her that the client's name is "Blair," not "Claire"), the gravity of the message (e.g., having a challenging performance conversation or sharing the exciting news of a promotion may be best done in person, and video is the next best option), and the level of specificity and actionability of the feedback (e.g., a series of edits to make in a Word document may be easiest to implement and track when provided via email or using the comments feature of the application).

Frances, a partner with a law firm in Paris, relies heavily on feedback provided via email and via the "track changes" and comments tools in written documents. The comments feature in Microsoft Word allows her to provide targeted, specific feedback to her associates that they can immediately integrate into a document. This feature allows her to provide both the corrections and some explanation for the changes to help her associates learn. Frances also shared a story of a very senior attorney providing her with feedback that left a lasting mark on her career:

> When I just started working as an associate in my firm I received very generous feedback from a senior partner at another firm we were collaborating with. I was leading a lot of high level, technical work – finance, paperwork, etc. One afternoon I sent a very long email to everyone on the team, and this senior partner wrote back to me – and only me, not copying everyone else – offering some corrections, but not in a critical way. He was not someone who would normally give me feedback – I didn't work directly for him and he has many demands on his time. But he could see that I needed some help on a few very specific things, and I wasn't getting the support I needed from my own leadership. Although his feedback was framed really positively, I still had an immediate reaction of anxiety – like I had done something wrong. As I had time to think about his feedback I felt very grateful for it. I appreciated that he didn't copy everyone else on the email, and that he provided specific edits and examples. I used his feedback for a long time to strengthen my work going forward.

Although elements of written feedback can be easily misinterpreted (e.g., tone), one advantage of written feedback is the discretion and "space" it provides. If a colleague sends feedback via email, I have the choice of reading it now and coming back to review it again later, or ignoring it for a while and reading it when I'm ready. Feedback in written documents – such as comments on a draft presentation or report – can be wonderfully specific and easy to act on. When done well, the feedback recipient is able to see exactly what portion of the document the feedback is referring to, and may be able to easily incorporate that feedback into the document. They can also take their time reviewing and thinking about the feedback before acting on it. Texts and chats, on the other hand, can feel intrusive and harder to control. The immediacy and in-your-face alerts of texts or instant messages can convey urgency, making them harder to ignore until later. This immediacy can be useful when quick, just-in-time feedback helps us to quickly adjust our behavior, but it also makes the context much harder to control.

One challenge with fast technology, like emails and texting, is that firing off a quick note is very easy, and doesn't require deep thought and planning. Before firing off a quick feedback note, think about the experience of the recipient. Where will they be when they receive your text or email? Is it really so urgent that you need to tell them right now? What could be misconstrued by the lack of tone and context in your message?

When a feedback recipient has self-control, self-discipline, and is able to recognize their own emotional reactions and need to pause, feedback via email or text can be very effective. Although a text or email from a colleague or friend could interrupt your day at any time, a feedback recipient who recognizes that they own 50% of the feedback exchange also recognizes that they have no obligation to respond immediately. In fact, feedback provided via email can be most effective when the recipient takes the time to read the feedback, allow their immediate emotional reaction to occur, and then walk away to get the space to mindfully process and think about the feedback before responding. For instance, under the right circumstances (e.g., emotional maturity, a trust-based working relationship), a manager may choose to send an employee their written performance review a few hours before their annual performance discussion. This allows the employee to read the feedback on their own, to work through immediate emotional reactions, to have time to cool off, and to formulate questions and ideas for follow-up in the performance conversation that will happen later in the day.

Technology-enabled feedback can drive immediate behavior change and course correction. For example, new innovations in classroom technology enable teachers to receive immediate feedback on their classroom behavior and to make changes in the moment to provide better instruction and to improve the classroom environment. Several studies have leveraged cameras in the classroom that enable a teaching coach in another room to observe a class in real time and provide feedback directly into a teacher's ear via Bluetooth technology (Rock, Gregg, Thead, Acker, Gable, & Zigmond, 2009; Rodgers, Kennedy, VanUitert, & Myers, 2019). Rock and colleagues found that immediate, specific, and positively framed corrective (aka negative) feedback resulted in improved teaching techniques, a better classroom climate, and even improved student behavior. Teacher self-awareness and learning also improved when journal reflection was coupled with the in-ear feedback. When asked if the "bug-in-ear" technology was distracting, the majority of teachers indicated that they were able to focus on their teaching while also attending to the occasional feedback from their observer coach. When I read this research, I was immediately taken back to the early 2000s MTV dating show "Taildaters," where a contestant on the show would go on a blind date and receive real-time in-ear feedback from friends or family members, who were watching the entire date on a webcam. It's not clear whether this strategy works effectively for dating, but fortunately it has been shown to be highly effective in teaching contexts.

Overall, feedback provided via technology can be both extremely helpful and also extremely ineffective, depending on the situation. Feedback providers have even more responsibility to consider the context and impact of their chosen medium when leveraging technology for feedback. Questions to help drive this decision include:

- How essential is it that this feedback be provided immediately?
- Will immediate delivery of this feedback (e.g., via text or instant message) help the person? Are they in a situation where they can or need to apply it immediately?
- Will advanced written feedback (e.g., an email) provide this person with the time and space to read and reflect on the feedback, and therefore lead to a more effective follow-up conversation later?
- What could this person be doing right now that I could be interrupting with my phone call, text, or Slack message?
- How much will this feedback be enriched by videoconference, where he/she can see my expression and body language, and vice versa?

When in doubt, ask the other person how they prefer to receive feedback. Taking time to understand individual preferences can lead to a more tailored, more personal, more effective interaction, and can also help to build the relationship for the long-term.

Tech that Supports and Encourages Feedback

The last decade has seen a rise in tools that make giving, receiving, and asking for feedback easier and less threatening. By creating an ecosystem intended specifically for the exchange of feedback, tools like Quantum Workplace, Culture Amp, and Lattice enable colleagues to freely exchange feedback whenever they choose. These platforms provide an invitation and a safe space to ask for and provide feedback, since the exchange of feedback is the primary purpose of the tools. Tools like Quantum Workplace also provide just-in-time guidance on best practices, such as being specific, that prompt feedback providers to give higher-quality feedback. By using one of these platforms, individuals are empowered to pose questions to colleagues at any time – such as in the midst of or at the conclusion of a project, before or after an annual review, or simply at a moment when they are looking for input or someone to "hold up the mirror." Posing simple questions, like "What is one thing I should stop, start, and continue doing on this project to be a more effective contributor?" enables the individual to get valuable, specific, actionable inputs from colleagues who, in turn, feel permission to provide their perspective and advice.

Adam, the Global Leader of Learning and Talent at a large multinational commercial real estate organization, shared an example of rolling out an informal feedback platform. The idea of the platform was to provide employees with a way to give and ask for feedback throughout the year, solely for development. The feedback would never inform the annual review cycle, which, up until then, was generally the only time employees received feedback. Despite an appetite for more feedback, Adam found that deploying a tool like this requires careful change management in order to succeed. Says Adam,

> Organizationally, there was not a strong feedback culture. People were very nervous about how the feedback would be used. Even though they were told feedback was only for development, was provided only to them, and would not impact ratings or promotions, they didn't believe or trust it. They viewed it with skepticism. We needed to invest more in change management for rolling out a tool like this – you can't just put it out there and expect people to start using it. If employees did use it to give and ask for feedback, we could really shift our feedback culture. It's a chicken and egg question. What comes first – the feedback culture that gets people to use the tools, or getting people to use the tools in order to elevate the feedback culture?

User-driven feedback tools empower individuals to choose when they receive feedback, from whom, and what they want the feedback to focus on (Young & McCauley, 2019). A hybrid of pulse surveys (quick and easy to distribute and to respond to) and 360/multisource feedback surveys (aggregating input from a variety of sources), user-driven feedback tools put leaders or users in the driver's seat of requesting feedback from colleagues. These tools may include quantitative questions (e.g., pre-written items that users respond to on a seven-point scale), or open-ended qualitative questions where respondents provide written feedback on the leader's topics of choice. Young and McCauley note that one important feature of user-driven feedback tools, like any 360 feedback tool,[1] is that responses are not linked back to feedback providers. Although a user will know who they requested feedback from, they should not be able to attribute specific responses or comments back to any individual. When providing feedback through tools like 360s, raters are more likely to be honest and candid when their anonymity is assured (Bracken, Timmreck, Fleenor, & Summers, 2001). For balanced and honest feedback, user-driven feedback-seeking tools should require a minimum number of raters in order to protect the confidentiality of the respondents and also to prevent any one voice from dominating the tone of the feedback.

Feedback received from user-driven tools can lead to increased self-awareness and accountability for results, greater learning and development, and higher levels of engagement (Wiita, 2018; Young & McCauley, 2019). Putting the feedback tool in the hands of the user enables them to receive feedback that will help them assess progress toward their goals. In other words, these tools provide data on the gap between the user's current state of performance, and their desired goal state. Users can seek true process feedback at the time and on the topics of their choosing, and then immediately integrate the most useful insights from the feedback into their behavior.

Tech-Generated Feedback

Not only does technology give us tools and platforms to provide feedback to others person to person, it can also provide feedback *directly* to users. Devices like smart phones, Apple Watches, Fitbits, Oura Rings, Whoop straps, and Garmin devices track our steps, inactivity, heart rate, and sleep patterns, among other things. These devices open up access to critical data and biofeedback that increase our awareness around our physical health and the impact of our lifestyle choices. Research by Fox and Duggan (2012) found that 69% of US citizens track at least one health behavior with some kind of wearable tech. Wearable tech provides real-time feedback that enables immediate course correction and behavior change. I recently noticed that, throughout the day, a colleague kept suddenly sitting up and improving her posture. At one point I asked her if she was okay, and she showed me a device on her back that connected to her iPhone and alerted her when she was slouching and needed to sit upright. In another meeting, I watched a friend stand up and walk around the table every 30 minutes. The Fitbit on their wrist vibrated every 30 minutes when they were sedentary, to remind them to stand up and move around.

In addition to wearable tech, hundreds of apps and programs for smart phones, tablets, and computers provide real-time feedback and goal tracking with a little bit of input. A friend recently told me about a diet app on her phone that is helping her to stay motivated and make lasting changes. She established goals for weight loss, exercise, and diet, and uses the app to track her progress toward those goals,

> I put in what I eat and my exercise and the app gives me feedback on how I'm doing. It gives me positive feedback every few weeks about my successes and shows me how I'm tracking against my goals. It also provides short-term reinforcement. If I eat 3 vegetables in one day I get a dancing broccoli icon, thumbs up for drinking enough water, and also immediate feedback on foods I'm eating that are not very healthy. This feedback has helped me learn a lot about the health value of the foods I'm eating. I've always had trouble sticking to a diet but this one is fun and helps me stay motivated. I can track how I'm doing against my goals and get immediate reinforcement. This is the first time I've ever been able to be on track with a diet … but really it's not just a diet. This app has helped me build new habits and truly change my lifestyle.

When she told me about this app, I gushed about the magic of control theory. The app helps her track her progress toward closing in on her goals, and ongoing feedback about her behavior tells her what she's doing right and what she can do differently to further close the gap between her current state and her goals.

Hermsen, Frost, Renes, and Kerkhof (2016) conducted a meta-analysis[2] of 69 studies on feedback from technology and behavior change. They found that feedback via technology platforms or apps led to a wide array of meaningful behavior changes, including, among other things:

- Eating more fruit
- Eating less, overall
- Increased physical activity
- Safer driving behavior
- Better posture
- Reduced screen time
- Weight loss
- Reduced electricity consumption
- Using less water via shorter showers

Each of these behaviors was considered a habit. Habits are formed when a stimulus/response pattern is developed, and we sometimes act without full awareness. These authors found that immediate or real-time feedback via technology is valuable because it disrupts that stimulus/response cycle and calls our awareness to our behavior. With this newfound awareness, it's easier to make intentional choices about our behavior. Feedback is often used to reflect on past behavior in order to improve future behavior, but Hermsen and colleagues noted that immediate feedback has the power to make us pause in the midst of a behavior, become more aware, and deliberately choose a different behavior.

Performance feedback provided directly from technology can also boost job performance. Organizations are increasingly adopting tools and technology that enable tracking of employees' activities and performance. Bernstein and Li (2017) found that employees believe that evidence-based tech-generated performance data is more transparent. It enables real-time feedback that is specific, objective, and devoid of emotion, since it is provided directly from technology and not a manager or colleague. Bernstein and Li found that when employees are provided with system-generated feedback that tells them how they are tracking against goals or standards, they engage in fewer nonproductive activities and achieve higher performance. These gains were even higher for employees who perceive low support from their managers and who care little about social comparison. The ability to get straightforward, task-focused performance feedback without engaging with their manager or peers empowered these employees to make better use of their time and to increase their productivity.

Research has only scratched the surface on the impact, benefits, and downsides of tech-enabled feedback. Constant alerts, notifications, and feedback prevent us from being present, focused, and getting into flow. These distractions pull us away from whatever we are doing and may provide feedback on something that's not presently our highest priority. It's also possible that too-frequent increments of feedback get in the way of seeing the big picture or meaningful progress on goals. Noticeable progress toward our goals is essential in order to stay motivated to pursue our goals (aka the "rate of discrepancy reduction" in control theory; Carver & Scheier, 1998). When effort is being exerted to attain a goal, feedback increments should be long enough that progress is discernable. For instance, when trying to lose weight, a weekly weigh-in will show more substantial progress than a daily weigh-in, where progress will be minimal and less inspiring. When progress occurs quickly and feedback indicates tangible movement toward goals, we tend to become more motivated to persist toward those goals. On the other hand, slow or no progress has a commensurate demotivating effect – resulting in negative emotions and reduced motivation to persist (Chang, Johnson, & Lord, 2010). Even worse, if progress shows that we are moving in the *opposite* direction to our goals, motivation plunges further, alongside our expectations of successfully achieving our goals. When it comes to tech, set your notifications and alerts to an appropriate increment that will help you see meaningful progress.

Box 3.1 Internet Trolls

It's hard to have a discussion of online feedback and reviews without considering the behavior of internet trolls. Bishop (2013) defines internet trolling as "the posting of provocative or offensive messages on the internet" (p. xiii), often for the sake of intentionally abusing another person or in an attempt to have a humorous effect. Discussion forums or comment threads have the potential to facilitate meaningful dialogue and feedback on others' ideas and contributions. These forums are also fertile ground for unconstructive, unproductive, and, at times, hurtful comments from posters hiding behind the veil of anonymity that the internet provides. For example, if Rachid writes an article for his local newspaper about charter schools, he might be devastated to find hurtful, mean, and personal comments about him and his ideas in the reader comments. Recent research has begun to explore what motivates people to engage in troll-like behavior. Negative mood, a negative context, and seeing others' negative, hurtful posts all increase the likelihood that a person will post troll-like comments or feedback in an online forum (Cheng, Bernstein, Danescu-Niculescu-Mizil, & Leskovec, 2017). A key takeaway of this book is that you cannot control the feedback or comments that others provide to you, but you can control how you respond to them. In the example of Rachid, he has several choices for how to handle the hurtful comments on his article. He can read each one and take it to heart, including comments that are an unfounded attack on his personality or character, interpreting each comment as feedback on his behavior and ideas. Or, he could read the comments out of curiosity, all the while staying mindful that the commenters are strangers and may lack some of the essential attributes of good feedback providers: Expertise, trust, and credibility. He could choose to screen for comments that are actually useful – those that will help him build on his ideas or expand his thinking on charter schools, and take those as useful feedback. Undoubtedly Rachid will have a strong emotional reaction to the negative comments. Regardless of how he chooses to respond to and accept the comments, he will want to allow time for his initial emotional reactions to pass first! Firing back an emotionally charged reaction will likely provoke further unproductive dialogue.

Indirect Feedback Driven by Tech

In 1995, online auction site eBay introduced a feature that would fundamentally shift the way consumers interact with businesses. Ebay's feedback system enabled never-before-seen transparency between buyers and sellers and is credited with driving eBay's success when compared to its competitors (Tadelis, 2016). This simple and transparent feedback system is now a standard feature on online commerce sites. As a result, a new form of indirect feedback has introduced challenges for businesses, an outlet for both delighted and unhappy consumers, and transparency and trust for buyers.

Person-to-person transactions on eBay work because of trust and reputation. A seller on eBay builds their reputation and earns the trust of future buyers by getting high ratings (on a positive, neutral, and negative "star" scale) and specific, positive comments from past buyers and transactions. What is new and game-changing about this approach is that the seller is the target of the feedback, but the feedback is written for future buyers. Compared to a traditional feedback exchange where the target and the audience are the same person (the feedback recipient), this new feedback "triangle" is more complex.

Other online and app-based businesses have adopted similar models of consumer feedback. Amazon uses a five-star rating system coupled with text-based reviews, and allows users to rate the helpfulness of each review – creating a rating system

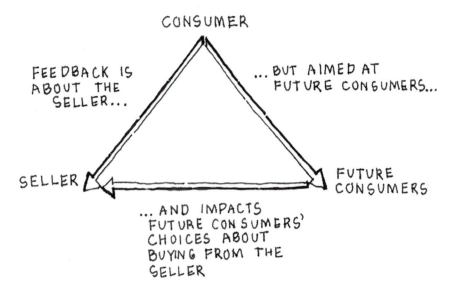

Figure 3.2 Indirect feedback via technology creates a complex communication triangle.

for ratings! Unlike Amazon, where consumers are rating products, eBay ratings tend to focus more on the actual seller – the effectiveness of their communication, the timeliness and quality of their shipping, and their honesty in describing the product (Tadelis, 2016). The stakes are higher with eBay ratings because the reputation of the seller, built through aggregate ratings and user feedback, has a significant impact on future sales. Amazon has the luxury of discontinuing sales of a product when it has a pattern of low ratings. The reputation risk is absorbed by the specific product rather than by Amazon as the seller. Rideshare apps like Uber also leverage both passenger and driver ratings and feedback to ensure the quality of their services. After completing a trip, passengers rate drivers on a scale of 1–5 and provide specific comments or compliments directly back to the driver. The driver's average rating dictates the number and quality of future opportunities. Specifically, the higher a driver's rating, the earlier "right of refusal" he or she gets to a new passenger pickup. Highly rated drivers get first pick of highly rated passengers. Passenger ratings work the same way. After each trip, drivers rate their passengers on a 1–5 scale but do not have the option to provide comments or compliments to passengers. Drivers can see passengers' aggregate ratings and choose whether or not to accept the trip. These ratings made by both drivers and passengers create feedback on "performance" as a passenger or a driver, inform future riders/drivers about what to expect, and – most importantly – dictate future experiences and opportunities.

These new, highly transparent rating systems are valuable to consumers looking to make an informed purchase or have a desirable experience. They create accountability and motivation for sellers and businesses to provide high-quality products and services and take care of their customers. However, they can also rob businesses of the opportunity to course correct for disappointments or problems. This complex triangle of indirect feedback actually undermines the value of timely, direct feedback. Sure, businesses can identify patterns of failure or opportunities that surface through customer feedback over time, but the indirect and often delayed nature of feedback on platforms like Yelp prevent businesses from taking immediate action.

For example, Alex, who manages a Michelin-starred restaurant, has set up an exceptional system for patrons to provide feedback on their dining experience. Staff at the restaurant ask guests for feedback on their food after every course. If staff members notice an unfinished dish or a drink pushed aside, they ask guests for feedback specifically on that item and offer something different on the house if the guest was disappointed or unsatisfied. Dining guests receive comment cards with their bill. At the end of the meal, they are asked by staff about their overall experience. Shortly after dining they receive an online rating form (a 1–5 star scale plus ratings on specific dimensions and open-ended comments) via email or a reservation app. And yet, despite all of these opportunities, guests will take to the very public postings of online sites like Yelp and Tripadvisor to rave or rant about their visit, without ever mentioning a word of dissatisfaction during the dining experience. Says Alex,

> The challenge with Yelp restaurant reviews is that guests don't have to give direct feedback or confront the real issues. And as a result, they don't give you a chance to fix the situation. When I read negative Yelp reviews, rarely did those guests actually share feedback directly with us. They go online to complain about things that we didn't even know about – like didn't get a birthday dessert, yet they never told anyone it was their birthday. The problem with online reviews is that people who post have no accountability. It's too late for us to do anything. They had ample opportunities to provide feedback while they were dining with us. We want our guests to have a wonderful experience, and we want to fix something that's not meeting their expectations. Why wait to do this indirect feedback where no action can be taken?

Parker, who owns a yoga studio, has had similar experiences with online reviews.

> Someone posted feedback about one of our teachers, who is an older man, in an online review. The person – we'll call him Mr. X – who posted the review was planning to attend class with a friend. Unfortunately the friend was over 20 minutes late to this one-hour class. The door was already locked, and the teacher did not let the friend in. Mr. X left a disgusting review on Yelp that attacked our teacher's character and age, and said he'd only come back to the studio if the owners fired him. Luckily we were able to get Yelp to take down the review as it was ageist and discriminatory.

Online reviews like these are clear examples of outcome feedback. They provide a summary view of what an experience was like, and leave no window to address the feedback and course correct. Research by Cabral and Hortacsu (2010) found that after their first bad review, online auction sellers experience a 13% drop in sales. Similarly, Luca (2016) found that an additional star in a Yelp rating (a 1–5 star scale) equates to a 5–9% increase in revenue. According to Yelp's website, 92 million unique visitors use the site *each month* to leverage or post one of their nearly 200 million reviews. The indirect feedback market is strong, which could be attributable to the sense of anonymity that feedback providers feel. In an earlier discussion about 360 feedback, rater anonymity was highlighted as a critical factor for honest and candid rater feedback (Bracken et al., 2001). Despite opportunities to provide direct feedback in dining or shopping situations, consumers who are uncomfortable providing feedback may gravitate toward the indirect feedback option.

Although indirect feedback may be frustrating for businesses, the themes and patterns that emerge from aggregating consumer feedback in online reviews can highlight important needs and opportunities for businesses. A study by Ranard, Werner, Antanavicius, Schwartz, Smith, Meisel, Asch, Ungar, and Merchant (2016) found that Yelp reviews of hospitals uncovered important dimensions of patient care that hospitals were not evaluating. These researchers found that Yelp reviews were highly correlated with traditional patient feedback surveys ($r = .50$), but also discovered 12 new categories that were not included on those traditional surveys, such as the cost of the hospital visit, staff compassion, care for visiting family members, the experience with billing and insurance, scheduling, and facilities. In short, reviewing online feedback in aggregate (to avoid over-indexing on individual, dissatisfied customers) can help businesses identify criteria and dimensions that are important to consumers that they are not currently attending to.

There's More to Learn

Technology has changed, and will continue to change, the way we give feedback to one another, the way we receive feedback from our environments, and the opportunities that others have to respond to and use that feedback. Unsurprisingly, "real life" is unfolding much faster than research can keep up. Tech companies and research institutions have massive opportunities to further investigate the role that technology is playing in our human interactions. I'll be the first to admit that feedback is only one small niche in that universe, albeit an important one that impacts our relationships, the success or failure of businesses and individuals tied to those businesses, and how we think about ourselves in relation to others and the world around us.

Try It

Next time you are prompted to provide feedback on a service, experience, or product using technology – such as an app, online review, or third-party site – pause to think about who is on the other end of it. Imagining another person on the other side of online interactions isn't always intuitive but, inevitably, another human will be impacted – positively or negatively – by your feedback. Apply your feedback best practices even in these seemingly anonymous encounters. Chapter 4 will give you some immediately actionable tools and practices to apply.

Looking for More?

After scrolling through Facebook or reading online reviews or – worse yet – comments on newspaper articles, you may feel a little deflated. Develop your grit in order to be more resilient to unconstructive online comments and reviews in the future. Angela Duckworth's great book *Grit: The Power of Passion and Perseverance* (2016) digs into what grit is, why it matters, and how to cultivate it.

Notes

1 360 feedback tools enable individuals to get feedback from a variety of sources in one aggregated report. In a work context, these "raters" could include someone's manager(s), direct reports, peers, customers, and any other colleagues. Some assessments even allow input from friends and family members. 360s are very valuable because they help people compare their own self-ratings against the perceptions of others, who are often grouped into specific categories based on their relationship (e.g., all direct reports' ratings are averaged, all peers' ratings are averaged, etc.).

2 A meta-analysis is an aggregate study of many individual research studies. When findings are statistically significant in a meta-analysis, we can have confidence that those findings are meaningful, and not the result of a one-off study or idiosyncratic finding.

PART II

FEEDBACK BEST PRACTICES

CHAPTER 4

GIVE IT

The <u>absence</u> of feedback from a guest is meaningful feedback.
Alex, general manager of a Michelin-starred restaurant

I love feedback, I understand feedback, I see the value of feedback and how critical it is for high performance and goal achievement; I've studied and done work related to feedback for over 15 years. And yet, I sometimes find my own discomfort getting in the way of providing feedback. This makes me feel like a hypocrite, but it's also an important reminder that providing feedback, especially to people we care about, can be intimidating. We don't want to hurt their feelings, we don't want to seem critical or controlling, we may fear how they react, we may fear how they will judge us in return.

One day I was working in a shared office with a colleague who is also a great friend, and whom I admire and respect. She is also a very loud phone talker. I was having trouble concentrating and tuning out her conversation, despite my noise canceling headphones. When I had to take a phone call, my colleagues could not hear me over her voice. This was a great opportunity for real-time feedback – here we are, together in this room, she's loud talking, and because of our relationship I should be able to freely give her feedback. But, in reality, I was very uncomfortable addressing it with her. I was losing patience, didn't give the feedback much thought, and blurted out in a flurry of frustration, "Shhh Anna

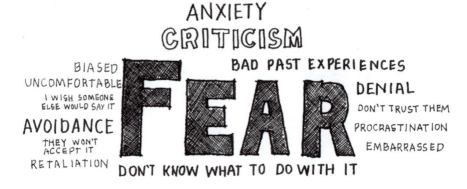

Figure 4.1 Common responses to how people feel about giving challenging feedback.

you are so loud! Please keep your voice down!" followed by an awkward laugh and averted eye contact. My feedback came across as snarky and emotionally charged. What went wrong? I allowed emotion and discomfort to get the best of me – I waited so long to give the feedback that I was exasperated, didn't pause to think about what I wanted to say or how I wanted to say it, and turned an inconsequential situation into an awkward and abrupt feedback dump that put some temporary strain on our relationship.

In a different situation, I took the time to think carefully about the feedback I wanted to give to a yoga teacher who routinely kept us 10–15 minutes past the scheduled 7:30am end time. This may not seem like a big deal, but when you have roughly 25–30 minutes after yoga to shower, get ready for work, and get out the door, 10–15 minutes makes a very big difference. I thought carefully about how I wanted to frame the feedback in a way that was objective and included the impact – why his behavior matters to me. One morning before class, I said to my teacher,

> Carlos, in the last few weeks most of our classes have gone past 7:30. I need to leave at 7:30 to get to work on time. If class is going to run long today, could you let us know when it's 7:30 so those of us who need to leave can quietly pack up?

Carlos laughed and said "I have a really hard time with time management." Class ended promptly at 7:30am that day and every day after. In this situation, compared to my terrible feedback delivery to Anna about her loud voice, I felt

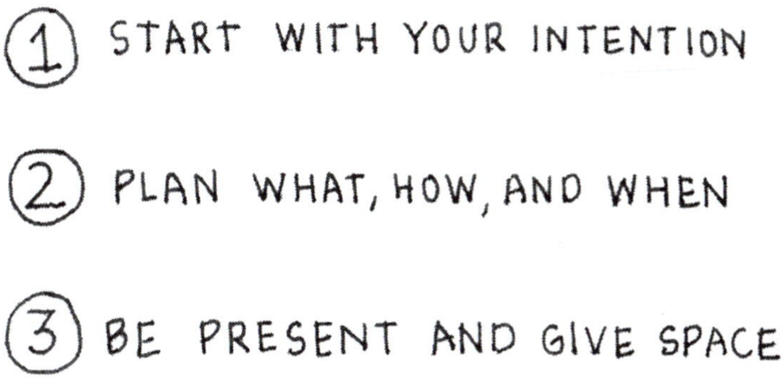

① START WITH YOUR INTENTION

② PLAN WHAT, HOW, AND WHEN

③ BE PRESENT AND GIVE SPACE

Figure 4.2 Three steps to setting the stage for effective feedback delivery.

comfortable providing feedback to Carlos because I used a few of my favorite feedback tricks, including:

- The Situation-Behavior-Impact (SBI) model
- Being clear about what "better" looks like
- Making my feedback forward-looking

Being a champion feedback provider isn't hard. Giving feedback can be intimidating and uncomfortable, but with a few key tools, sufficient practice, and a mindful mindset, anyone can become a feedback-giving guru. Drawing on the feedback best practices that we've learned in previous chapters, here are my three steps for creating a high-quality feedback exchange.

Start with Your Intention

Before you say anything, ask yourself: *Why am I giving this feedback?* Is your intention to be *right*? To make the other person feel small or foolish? To exert your power and dominance? Or is your intention to help this person to see a blind spot, to do something better next time, to learn and grow, to achieve their goals, or to have higher performance next time? The true value of feedback is in providing others with useful data on their behavior in order to help them to learn, to adjust their behavior, or to have greater self-awareness. Taking a control theory perspective, feedback is useful because it helps others to assess their current state with respect to their goals or desired state. Having a clear intention for whatever feedback you are preparing to give will help you decide what to say and how to say it. Having a "why" for your actions – a clear sense of purpose or objective – will make the interaction feel more constructive, productive, and authentic.

Your intention could be something like:

- I want Elijah to be aware of this blind spot because that awareness will improve his interactions with other colleagues
- I really like my hairstylist and want to continue coming to her but I need her to stop giving me crooked haircuts
- Adrienne's performance isn't meeting expectations and I want to address it now. Waiting will only make the inevitable conversation harder for both of us
- Oliver keeps doing this task wrong, but doesn't seem to realize it and no one else is telling him. I want to give him feedback so he'll know how to do it correctly going forward, so we won't have to do rework in the future, and so he doesn't look incompetent in front of our peers
- I am going to tell Candace she has spinach in her teeth because if the roles were reversed I would want her to tell me I had spinach in my teeth
- My teammate really shines when she is in the most challenging situations. It helps the rest of our team feel calm and rally together even in tough times. I don't think she realizes how much of a positive, inspiring effect she has on all of us, though – and I want to let her know

Taking a few minutes to check in with yourself, ask why you are giving this feedback and what you hope to achieve with it, will help you prepare for effective feedback delivery. Have clear purpose for your feedback, and feel more confident in the value of giving the feedback.

Plan What, How, and When

Once you have set your intention, map out exactly what you want to say, how you want to deliver it, and when. I'm amazed how many managers and team leaders in organizations don't take a few minutes to collect their thoughts before providing feedback to their teams or colleagues. Feedback will always be higher quality, clearer, and easier to use when a few minutes are invested to think through it in advance. Particularly with challenging or uncomfortable feedback, a few minutes spent planning, writing down, or saying aloud what you want to get across will ensure that you're saying what you really intend to say, you will surface anything that could be misconstrued or isn't clear, and will help you feel more comfortable giving the feedback.

What. The SBI model (Weitzel, 2000) can be particularly helpful here. The SBI model will help you plan out what you want to say and also ensure that the feedback recipient gets exactly the information that they need to use your feedback – the **situation** (S) where the behavior occurred, their specific **behavior** (B), and the **impact** (I) – and know why it matters. Using the SBI model to structure your feedback brings the situation to life again for the feedback recipient and also compels you to be evidence based in your feedback. Being evidence based in your feedback will help you to avoid making inaccurate or unfair assumptions about someone's behavior. How often do you find yourself making up stories about what's going on in someone else's head or concocting explanations for why they are behaving in a certain way?

One of my favorite theories in social psychology is the *fundamental attribution error* (Tetlock, 1985). When making sense of some experience or something that we have observed, other people stand out to us more than the situation that surrounds them. As a result, and because we are cognitively lazy, we tend to overestimate the influence of someone's personality and underestimate the role of the situation in explaining people's behavior. A classic example: When driving on the highway and someone speeds by or cuts you off, you may be tempted to say something along the lines of "what a jerk" or "that guy can't drive!" However, you know nothing about that other driver, and what he or she may be currently experiencing. Perhaps they are speeding to the hospital because a baby is on the way. Or racing to work because he or she is late for a critical meeting. None of these explanations rationalize bad driving – the point is that just because someone makes one dumb move doesn't mean that they are a jerk or a bad driver. The other person may be kind, cautious, trustworthy, honest, and have a great driving record, but *the power of the immediate situation* is influencing their driving behavior at this very moment.

Using the SBI model and remaining evidence based will help you avoid making assumptions about *why* the other person behaved the way they did. You will undoubtedly have hypotheses about their behavior, but remember that no matter how hard you try you simply cannot see into their minds. Even if you are *right* in your assumptions about the other person, they are more likely to get defensive or deny your feedback if there is not objective evidence to support your points. When you focus on observable behaviors – things that you saw with your own eyes or heard with your own ears – the feedback is stronger, less likely to be refuted, and will also prevent you from getting into an ugly and unwinnable debate about what is happening inside someone's head. Remember, the most effective feedback always focuses on someone's behavior or the task, not the *person*. The SBI model will help you to stay focused on observable behaviors and to steer clear of uncomfortable inferences about someone's motivations, intentions, abilities, or personality. It's much easier to change your behavior than it is to change who you are as a person.

Framing your feedback as forward-looking can also ease the discussion. Feedback can be frustrating to receive because it is, by definition, backward-looking. You can't change what has happened in the past, which is why feedback often elicits negative reactions ranging from apathy to defensiveness to anger. Because they can't undo their past behavior, feedback recipients may feel criticized, judged, or even helpless by the feedback that you provide. Feedback becomes instantly less painful and more useful when we simply add a forward-looking lens. We can use feedback on past events as data points to inform future behavior. After all, the purpose of feedback is to help people to learn, or to do more of something, less of something, or something different altogether in the future, that will be more effective than whatever they have done in the past.

Box 4.1 Radical Candor

Many organizations have weak feedback environments where feedback is not openly exchanged, valued, or used. However, in some organizations, the pendulum has swung in the opposite direction as they embrace the concept of *radical candor*. Authors Vich and Kim (2016) define radical candor as "proactive and compassionate engagement in an unpleasant and direct feedback process" (p. 12). In her book, Kim Scott (2015) suggests that radical candor exists at the intersection of *caring personally* and *challenging directly*. These two elements are essential for making feedback clear and direct, but without coming across as uncaring and aggressive. In his *Principles* (2017), Ray Dalio, founder of hedge fund Bridgewater Associates, espouses a constant exchange of feedback and evaluating *accurately, not kindly*, because "accurate criticism is more valuable" than compliments (p. 428). Dalio attributes much of his company's success to their culture of transparency and accountability, which is enabled by the open exchange of candid feedback. Both of these perspectives – radical candor and Dalio's "tough love" approach to feedback – are consistent with the feedback best practices outlined in this book: Giving timely, specific, direct, actionable feedback without sugarcoating it. What's important to remember is that too much negative feedback can completely overwhelm the recipient (Smither & Walker, 2004), leading them to disengage rather than to use feedback for higher performance. Before applying practices like radical candor and transparency, consider the context (What kind of feedback environment am I in? How will I be violating norms by providing this kind of feedback?) and the individual (What kind of feedback orientation does this person have? Do they love and seek out feedback, or freeze up and shut down when they receive it?). Moving to a culture of total candor and transparency will take time as people adjust to new behaviors, norms, and expectations.

You can direct the focus of your feedback toward the future by either a) offering guidance on applying the feedback to a future situation or b) by taking a coaching approach and asking an open-ended question to help the recipient think through the "next time" opportunity. For example, my two favorite teenagers, Nia and Justice, shared examples of forward-looking feedback exchanges that make feedback easier to receive and apply. Nia spoke of her band teacher, who consistently communicates with Nia and her classmates in a caring, positive, and inspiring way. When he gives them feedback on their playing he "tells us specific things we can try or do differently next time we play a song." Similarly, Justice spoke of a teacher who is a great listener and talks to students like adults, giving them ownership for their choices and their behavior. Justice also shared an example of a schoolwork discussion with her mom. When Justice received grades that didn't meet her expectations, her mom helped her use that feedback for good by "thinking through ways to do things differently going forward – such as study habits, how I'm approaching the work or spending my time." This forward-looking discussion lifted Justice out of a defensive or emotional state and into a problem-solving mode to figure out how to have improved grades next time.

A forward-looking lens on feedback can help to "broaden and build" (Fredrickson, 2001) the recipients' emotional reactions and creative problem-solving in response to negative feedback. Rather than get defensive, dwell in negative emotions, or push back on the feedback, a recipient who is encouraged to think about what they will do next time the situation occurs may be more likely to accept and use the feedback. Positive psychology techniques like Appreciative Inquiry and visualization can help with processing feedback and thinking through how to use it in detail (O'Malley & Gregory, 2011). Like coaching, Appreciative Inquiry uses thoughtful questions to draw out the other person's ideas about what could be possible in the future, in a nonjudgmental way (Cooperrider & Srivastva, 1987). Visualization encourages the feedback recipient to get concrete and specific about what they will do in the future, and even activates the same neural networks that are activated when engaging in the actual behavior (O'Malley, Ritchie, Lord, Gregory, & Young, 2009;

Ungerleider, 2005). Visualization, and its impact on important neural pathways, has been shown to drive higher performance for athletes and activate positive emotions that lead to improved performance in the workplace (Kauffman, 2006; Ungerleider, 2005). Questions as simple as, "When you present on next month's investor call, what will you do differently?" and "What will that really look and feel like?" can shift feedback recipients out of an emotional downward spiral and into a constructive, future-focused, problem-solving mode following negative feedback. You may not have a time machine, but you can provide the next best thing by giving the feedback recipient a chance for a "do-over" when your feedback is forward-looking and future-focused.

How and When. Once you know what you want to say, figure out the most effective medium for your message and when to deliver it. As a feedback provider you have many options for how and when to provide feedback. You can give feedback face-to-face – in person or using a videoconference. You can give feedback verbally over the phone, or in writing via email or text (or the myriad of other messaging options – instant messaging, Slack, Facebook messaging, etc.). You can choose to give the feedback right away, or delay hours, days, or weeks. You can provide feedback in a private and confidential setting, or in the company of others. You can even provide feedback on public fora such as YouTube or Yelp, or countless other websites and applications.

Research from the early 2000s found that verbal feedback was still the most commonly used method of delivering feedback, but is actually most effective when paired with something in writing or a visual (Alvero, Bucklin, & Austin, 2001; Au & Chan, 2013). Each method of providing feedback has advantages and disadvantages. Feedback delivered face-to-face – whether in person or via video – enables both the feedback provider and the recipient to see each other's facial expressions and body language, which are important when the feedback may evoke strong emotions. On the other hand, research has shown that feedback providers tend to be more lenient and less direct when giving negative feedback face-to-face, as opposed to in writing (Waung & Highhouse, 1997). Their discomfort giving negative feedback face-to-face results in the message being watered down.

Feedback provided via email tends to be the second most preferred method for receiving feedback (Au & Chan, 2013). One advantage of email-based feedback is that it can be immediate, yet the recipient has some discretion and control over when and where they choose to read it and take action. Text or instant message-based feedback, on the other hand, conveys an immediacy and can be more intrusive than email-based feedback. Texts and instant messages are more conducive to shorter messages, too, and are therefore best suited to quick, just-in-time or in-the-moment feedback about relatively inconsequential topics.

For example, if I were at a party and had spinach in my teeth, I would prefer my friend at the party to tell me face-to-face once we get a private moment. If that wasn't possible, a quick, discreet text would let me take immediate action. Email would be unhelpful – I wouldn't plan to check my email at a party and would probably find out long after the party, which would only leave me feeling foolish about the spinach that was in my teeth all night. In another situation, however, when a client let me know that we did not succeed in securing a new piece of work with them, I appreciated a phone call to share the news and some detailed feedback about why. A text would have felt flippant and dismissive; an email would have felt impersonal. A face-to-face conversation wasn't realistic with the geographic constraints.

The same goes for positive feedback. When sharing very exciting positive news or praise, think about the medium that will best convey the message. Letting someone know that they got promoted via text may feel anticlimactic. A face-to-face discussion could make the news seem all the more exciting and honorable (via video if in person is not realistic). On the other hand, if you work on a remote team and want to let a team member know what a great job they did on a big virtual presentation, a quick instant message or email will provide the timely reinforcement that would get lost if you waited to have a face-to-face conversation.

Timing can make or break feedback delivery. In general, the sooner feedback is provided after the focal "event," the better. The longer that you wait, the more the memory of the event fades in both your mind and the mind of the feedback recipient. The sooner feedback is delivered the more likely that people are to pay attention to it, and also to act on it (van der Kleij, Eggen, Timmers, & Veldkamp, 2012). Sharing feedback soon after the event also shows that you care. Waiting days or weeks to share feedback sends a message to the recipient that this isn't a priority for you. Remember, the one caveat to giving feedback as soon as possible is waiting until you are in the right setting. Most people are very uncomfortable receiving feedback in a public setting, in front of others. Delay your feedback delivery until you can be in a private setting, particularly when the feedback is negative or might make the recipient feel embarrassed. Positive feedback and praise can be tricky – some people love to be praised in front of their peers or colleagues, whereas others will be completely mortified.

When deciding how and when to provide feedback, consider the significance and complexity of the feedback (minor issue or big deal?), how time-sensitive the feedback is (must know immediately versus okay to wait a few hours or a few days), and how likely the topic is to evoke strong emotions – particularly negative emotions (very straightforward and unemotional versus potentially charged, threatening, or challenging to work through?). Ultimately, the better you know the person that you are providing feedback to, the better able you will be to make smart choices about how and when to provide feedback. Also consider your own emotions and readiness to have the feedback discussion. If you feel hijacked, distracted, or unprepared, wait to give feedback when you can be present, calm, and focused.

Be Present and Give Space

At its core, feedback is a very human interaction. As a feedback provider, you have doubts, insecurities, fears, and assumptions that make giving feedback challenging. Feedback recipients have a similar set of fears, anxieties, doubt, and dread that have developed from years of unpleasant feedback exchanges. By connecting with one another as humans first, a feedback exchange can be easier and lead to meaningful changes in future behavior.

As a feedback provider, you not only choose when and how to deliver feedback, you also have control over the "human conditions" of the feedback exchange. One of the greatest gifts that you can give to the other person is your presence and full attention. Being fully mindful and present will not only enable you to be a great listener and ensure that the other person feels respected and heard, it will also help you to overcome any anxieties and self-doubts that you are having about the conversation. Mindfulness plays an important role in managing anxiety and reducing self-consciousness (Brown & Ryan, 2003), freeing up your consciousness to focus on the present situation, not your own doubts and fears.

Set yourself up for success by eliminating distractions that will get in the way of you being fully present. If possible, select a location where you can truly focus on the conversation – not in a busy common area or a "fishbowl" office where everyone who walks by catches your eye. Most of all, set your technology aside! Leave your phone in your bag or on your desk. Put it on "do not disturb" so you will not be distracted by it ringing or vibrating with calls, texts, or other notifications. Same with your computer or tablet. Research has shown that simply hearing your phone buzz – even if you don't look at the notification – distracts attention (Brown & Ryan, 2003). An interruption as simple as one text creates cognitive overload and divided attention that undermines our ability to stay present and focused in the conversation.

A colleague once shared a story with me about a feedback conversation that she had over the phone with her manager. Her manager had shared some constructive feedback with her – things that she could work on to be more effective in her role. She was reflecting on the feedback and talking about some of the challenges and self-doubts that were getting in her way, and in the background she could hear her manager typing on his computer. He was either distracted or attempting to multitask, but that one moment in their conversation deeply eroded her trust and respect for her manager. He was going through the motions of listening but was not actually present in the conversation. If you struggle with distraction or a temptation to multitask, do whatever necessary to create the right conditions for an effective conversation – meet in person, have a videoconference rather than a phone call, go to a different room where you will not be distracted by technology, other people, etc.

Being present and really listening means listening with your full attention to what the other person is saying, and paying attention to their body language, emotions, and expressions. Truly attentive, focused listening ensures that you pick up both what is being said and what is not being said, by attending to the words, tone, expressions, body language. Most people spend their days listening at "level 1," which is best described as self-focused listening. We hear what others say in relation to ourselves, rather than really hearing the other person (Whitworth, Kimsey-House, Kimsey-House, & Sandhal, 2009). For example, Asia gives her manager feedback that she thinks that their weekly team meetings could be more effective if they had a structured agenda. When Asia's manager responds, "You think our meetings are bad – you should see our monthly management meetings!" Asia does not feel heard, and instead feels that her manager deflected her feedback and tried to one-up her. This response may have been Asia's manager's attempt at empathy, connection, or humor but, ultimately, her response led to a missed opportunity to hear the feedback of a team member and to potentially act together to improve a work process. Asia's manager listened and responded at level 1 – she made it about herself, rather than about Asia's feedback and feelings.

Really listening means being fully present and focused on the other person and responding in a way that makes them feel heard and understood. Empathizing is an important part of a challenging feedback exchange and shows that you are truly listening and present. However, people often mistake empathizing for level 1 listening – giving an example or connecting back to their own experience rather than staying focused on the other person. Another common failed attempt at empathy is telling people how they should or should not feel. In an effort to put the other person at ease or to help them feel better, it's tempting to say "Oh, you shouldn't feel that way," but, in reality, this response simply discounts or minimizes how they actually feel. Rather, lean on your curiosity and coaching skills, "Tell me more about what makes you feel that way," or acknowledge their emotion, "Sounds like you are very frustrated by this situation."

Finally, give space. Receiving tough feedback requires both cognitive and emotional effort, and those two systems operate on different timelines. Emotional reactions occur much faster than our ability to rationally, cognitively process information. As a result, people need time to pause, process, and truly absorb the feedback that you've provided. This might require a pause in the conversation and a few moments of silence, which terrifies most people. But silence may simply mean that the other person is experiencing their immediate emotional reaction and taking time to actually process what you said. Therefore, don't get in their way! If you are uncomfortable with silence and tend to fill it with rambling and unnecessary talking, plan ahead to get out of your own way. When you need to give feedback that makes you a bit uncomfortable, pause to think about what you are going to say. Then say it. Then stop talking. Don't dig yourself into a hole by rambling on. Don't fill silence with words because you are uncomfortable with silence. More words are not better and, in fact, can lead people to feel unclear on what the issue is and as if they are being lectured.

What Happened Before, What Happens After

All feedback occurs in the context of a relationship. You may give feedback to someone you have worked or been friends with for 20 years, and that relationship will continue for another 20 years. You may provide feedback to someone you barely know, after a brief interaction. A bad feedback exchange could signal the end of a relationship. Honest, helpful feedback could initiate a relationship that will grow in the years to come. What you say, how you say it, and when you say it will elicit emotional and cognitive reactions from the feedback recipient that will shape not only how they perceive the feedback, but also how they perceive you and the relationship that you share.

Positive psychologist Barbara Fredrickson's (2013) research[1] has demonstrated that a positivity ratio of roughly 3:1 positive to negative emotions leads to happiness and thriving. This ratio also applies to relationships. Observe your feedback behavior with colleagues and family members. Does your feedback meet the 3:1 ratio? In other words, across all of your interactions with one person, have you had two to three positive interactions to buffer against every instance of negative feedback? Every interaction that you have with a person shapes how they will react to and behave in your next feedback exchange, and that feedback exchange, in turn, will impact the nature and tone of your interactions to come. Recall, that as a feedback provider, the recipient's perceptions of you impact how they hear your feedback. If they believe that you are credible, trustworthy, and know what you are talking about, they will be much more likely to accept and use feedback that you provide (Ilgen, Fisher, & Taylor, 1979). Developing your own sense of self-awareness will help you to better regulate your own behavior and how you show up in challenging conversations.

Finally, when making choices about when, where, and how to provide feedback, consider what you know about the feedback recipient. Practice empathy by putting yourself in their shoes. How are they experiencing the situation? What goals, fears, and concerns do they have? Based on your past interactions, when have you seen them handle feedback effectively? Finch, the wealth advisor we met in Chapter 2, puts herself in her clients' shoes before any interaction. She's learned that, in order to be effective:

> I have to tailor the feedback based on who I'm talking to. I have to understand their context – what challenges they have had in their life that have impacted their financial situation. I have to show empathy and show that I care. It's essential to acknowledge the fears, doubts, and assumptions that they have, and you only get to understand those by really getting to know your clients and building a relationship. Then we can give better advice because we have the context, the relationship, and the empathy. Knowing what's really happening with people and what they care about allows me to give the most useful feedback and advice.

Using best practices like making your feedback as specific as possible, being behavior-focused and evidence based, using the SBI model, and providing feedback in a timely manner are essential. But remembering that on the other side of every feedback exchange is another human with goals and fears and emotions will help you take your feedback skills to a higher level, and build stronger, trust-based relationships through your interactions.

Giving Feedback in Your Daily Life: What Will You Try?

Every day you are surrounded by opportunities to give high quality or thoughtless feedback, or to choose to withhold feedback that could be potentially useful and eye-opening to others (and maybe make your life easier). I asked a few friends and colleagues what feedback situations they find most vexing. Here are a few of my favorites, and some suggestions on how you might approach the situation.

Giving "upward" feedback to my boss. Power differentials also make feedback complicated. In general, people are more likely to withhold or water down negative feedback to those who they perceive to be in a position of power over them. They may fear retaliation or be held back by doubt in their own observations. When giving upward feedback, follow the same feedback best practices that you would in any other scenario. You might simply need to work on your confidence and muster up the courage to say what's on your mind. Take the time to plan out what you want to say. Check your intentions and why you want to provide this feedback in the first place. Many leaders live in a "feedback vacuum" – as they progress higher in their career they have fewer superiors and peers to provide them with candid feedback (Hall, Otazo, & Hollenbeck, 1999). Yet managers and leaders need feedback to grow, develop, and have increased self-awareness as much as anyone else. Like the celebrity magazines would say: *Bosses – they are just like us!*

Giving feedback to my teenager in a way that doesn't make her fly off the handle and slam her door. I have spent hundreds of hours teaching coaching skills to leaders and HR professionals, and one of my favorite observations from students is that adopting a coaching approach dramatically improves their communication with teenage children. By using a coaching approach, I mean asking open-ended questions and being nondirective, giving the other person ownership for coming up with a solution and moving forward with it. Next time you need to remind Khalil to put his shoes away, try giving him ownership and options for how he resolves the situation, rather than being directive. Rather than, "Khalil, I told you to put your shoes away. Put them away now," try,

> Khalil, when you leave your shoes in the middle of the living room floor it's really easy for others to trip over them. You can put your shoes anywhere you want, but out of the way. What would you like to designate as your shoe drop zone?

Giving a compliment that really has an impact on someone. When your BFF lands her dream job, your coworker crushes his presentation, or your local baker makes the best pastry you've ever tasted, use your feedback best practices to give a compliment that really means something. As we learned in Chapter 2, humans are hardwired to think in more detail and at a lower level of abstraction about negative situations, and think at a more general level when things are going well (Bodenhausen, Kramer, & Susser, 1994). This often shows up in the feedback that we give others. Whereas most people tend to be very detailed and specific in their negative feedback, positive feedback may be as general as "nice haircut," "great job on that presentation," or "Mmmm this is delicious." Compliments are more powerful and meaningful and can help people to identify good behaviors to repeat in the future when they follow feedback best practices – like being specific and behavior based. Instead of "congrats on your new job, Xena!" try, "Xena, you have worked so hard to develop as a leader and build your expertise in your field. You really earned this new role – I'm so proud of you!" Or, "Aaron, your presentation this morning was well organized, making it clear and easy to follow. You tied a lot of details together into a compelling story that made your points memorable and high impact." And, "Nelson, this kouign amann has the perfect consistency – it's crispy on the outside and gooey on the inside, and I love all of the cinnamon flavor." Finally, make sure the focus of your compliment is in the right place. For example, say "Amir you look fantastic in that dress!" (compliment Amir) as opposed to, "Amir that dress looks so good on you!" (complimenting the dress).

Being brave with negative feedback in service settings. You get a bad haircut, it feels easier to never go back to your hairstylist again than to share critical feedback about his or her handiwork.

Avoidance is always an option, but it doesn't fix the situation or help the other person to learn or grow. Applying feedback best practices – being specific, focusing on observable behavior or outcomes, framing feedback in terms of behavior, not the person, and being forward-looking – will make those tough feedback conversations in service settings a bit easier. Next time your haircut doesn't turn out the way you imagined, think about the outcome that would make you feel better: Do you want your stylist to fix it now? To cut it differently next time? To offer you a refund? Having clarity on what "good" looks like will help you ground your feedback. In Chapter 1, we learned that the real value of feedback is in helping you to gauge the distance between the current state and the desired state. So, if your current state (bad haircut) is far off from your desired state (good hair), what will it take to close that gap? And what is the timeline – is it today, or in six weeks during your next haircut? You can apply these same practices in other settings where the outcome hasn't been exactly what you were looking for – if your steak is overcooked at a restaurant, the clerk packs your bags too full at the grocery store, or if you feel like your primary care doctor isn't really listening to your questions and concerns. In that last example, you might say to your doctor,

Dr. Schein, when I asked you a question earlier about changing my diet, your answer was not as thorough as what I was looking for, and I felt a bit dismissed. I want to proactively manage my own healthcare and I would appreciate you spending more time and attention on my questions, particularly since I only see you once a year.

Finally ... Sandwiches Are for Eating, Not for Feedback

People often ask me if "the feedback sandwich" is a good practice – slipping negative feedback between two slices of positive feedback in order to "soften the blow" of the negative feedback. There is no research to support the effectiveness of this approach. Rather, the message tends to get lost or misconstrued. Feedback recipients leave the conversation feeling confused – was that just good or bad? – and unclear on what the real issue is and how they should take action. Worse yet, the more you practice the feedback sandwich, the more people around you will come to expect that any praise will be accompanied by negative feedback. Your positive feedback – which is important for building relationships and psychological safety – will instead come across as disingenuous, inauthentic, and a mere sugarcoating for the *real* message.

Try It

Today or tomorrow, identify an opportunity to give someone feedback and practice making it forward-looking. Think of feedback that you want to give to a colleague, friend or family member, or even the barista at the coffee shop. This doesn't need to be a complex or formal feedback opportunity – day-to-day, in-the-moment feedback works great. Instead of stopping with your traditional backward-looking feedback, add on a "Next time can you ..." or "What could you try differently next time?" at the end. Notice how it changes the dynamic of your feedback conversation.

Looking for More?

I'll admit, this is a departure from feedback, but if you are interested in developing your capacity for mindfulness and being present (which helps you be a better listener and a better partner in a feedback exchange), check out *Wherever You Go, There You Are* (1994) by Jon Kabat-Zinn. It's a seminal read on the habit and impact of practicing mindfulness.

Note

1 The efficacy and replicability of Fredrickson's research has been called into question, but her 2013 article showed continued support for the existence and importance of the positivity ratio.

CHAPTER 5

ASK FOR IT

The feedback evolves as the relationship evolves. As the relationship develops clients expect you to be the truth-teller. At the start of working with a new client, before you have the relationship, the trust, the relationship capital, the conversations tend to be lighter, sunnier. More candid feedback comes with increased trust and comfort on both sides. Established clients are more likely to give us feedback if there's something they don't like.

Finch, a Forbes Top 100 Women Wealth Advisor in the US

Imagine this scenario: You are sitting at your desk (or on your couch, or standing at the coffee bar, or wherever you operate on a daily basis) and a colleague, friend, family member, or partner comes around the corner and says, "[Your name here], I need to give you some feedback."

Close your eyes. Really imagine this situation. Use your best visualization skills. What does the setting look like? Who is the person giving you the feedback? Imagine their expression, their tone.

What's your immediate emotional reaction?

If you are like many people, it's negative. In previous chapters, we saw that people respond to this statement with reactions like, "brace yourself," "I steel myself to hear something negative," "duck and wait for criticism." Often, people feel like feedback is *happening to* them. It's not something that they asked for. It's presented at the time and place that's convenient for the provider, not when the recipient is ready, open, and interested in receiving the feedback. Unsolicited critical feedback can make you feel powerless – as if the feedback provider holds all of the power and control in the situation.

Getting beyond reactions like these (dread, bracing, expecting the worst, an amygdala hijack) requires a shift to an ownership mindset and a realization that, in any two-person feedback exchange, each person is 50% of the conversation. This powerless receiver mindset is likely shaped by years or decades of feedback interactions in which a person with power (a parent, teacher, coach, boss) approached feedback as a one-way, not-up-for-discussion transaction. Undoing this mindset – that feedback *happens* to you – requires a realization and acceptance that you ultimately have a choice in what you do with the feedback that others provide to you. As is the case with most human interactions, you cannot control others' behavior, but you can control how you respond and what you choose to do with their actions or words. In London and Smither's (2002) classic model of the feedback process, the delivery of feedback, the choice to accept that feedback, and the choice to actually *do* something with the feedback are three very distinct steps in the process, and the feedback recipient has full control over the choice to accept or use feedback.

How to Be a Great Feedback Recipient

You cannot control another person's behavior but you can control how you respond to it. In any feedback exchange, it's highly plausible that the person giving you feedback is not well versed in feedback best practices, is uncomfortable giving you feedback, and probably didn't take the time to think through, plan, and practice what they want to say. Therefore, it's highly plausible that in any feedback exchange, the person providing you with feedback will not clearly articulate what is really on their mind and may inadvertently say something that makes you feel a surge of emotion, some defensiveness, and confusion about the real issue and what you need to do about it.

In a situation like this you have choices. You can choose to be ruled by emotion, get defensive, reject the feedback, or exert your power by trying to make the feedback provider feel wrong, foolish, or guilty. Alternatively, you can assume positive intent, listen objectively, seek to understand what they are trying to communicate to you, and exert your power in the situation by asking clarifying questions and turning the exchange into an equal dialogue. As you can imagine, these two approaches result in extremely different outcomes – for both people involved and their relationship going forward, and also for actually doing something productive with the feedback. A feedback exchange that starts with discomfort and emotion can either escalate, or evolve into a collaborative and productive dialogue. It's important to recognize that the direction of the conversation is in the hands of both the feedback provider and the feedback recipient.

For example, Finch, the wealth advisor we've heard from in previous chapters, chose to stay calm, really listen, and seek to understand a client who gave her angry, critical feedback. A misunderstanding had occurred between Finch's team and the client. The client was known for being aggressive and having a temper and was not providing the feedback in a constructive way. Obviously angry, he yelled and hung up on a member of Finch's team. Finch proposed that they meet up in person for a follow-up conversation, which had the potential to be challenging. She had developed rapport with this client and was invested in maintaining their relationship and fixing the situation. She listened. She tried to take the emotion out of the conversation. Not only did she hear and accept the client's feedback, she also turned the conversation into a collaborative dialogue by providing feedback back to the client about his behavior. She suggested that next time he provide the feedback sooner rather than waiting, letting it build up, and having an angry outburst. Even though the conversation was uncomfortable, it advanced and changed the nature of their relationship to be more balanced, less one-sided. Later, the client shared with Finch that he respected the way that she had handled the situation by de-escalating it and giving him feedback on his own behavior.

Staying calm and overriding strong emotional reactions in challenging feedback situations is not easy. Accepting feedback with grace and cool emotions is easier

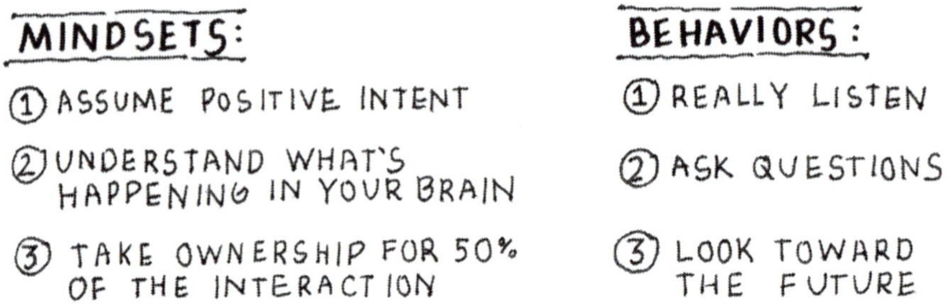

MINDSETS:

1. ASSUME POSITIVE INTENT
2. UNDERSTAND WHAT'S HAPPENING IN YOUR BRAIN
3. TAKE OWNERSHIP FOR 50% OF THE INTERACTION

BEHAVIORS:

1. REALLY LISTEN
2. ASK QUESTIONS
3. LOOK TOWARD THE FUTURE

Figure 5.1 Three mindsets and three behaviors to use to make receiving feedback more effective.

if you have a strong feedback orientation, healthy self-esteem, and an internal locus of control,[1] all of which can be strengthened and developed with time and effort. Regardless of where you stand on these dimensions, you can choose to practice a few mindsets and behaviors that will make these situations smoother and enable you to develop into a champion feedback recipient.

Mindsets[2]

The attitude, expectations, and state of mind that you bring to a feedback interaction will color your perceptions and influence your behavior. As we learned in Chapter 1, everyone has a feedback orientation – the way you think about, value, use, and actively seek out feedback (Linderbaum & Levy, 2010). Luckily, your feedback orientation is not fixed, and with effort and exposure to effective feedback interactions, you can develop and strengthen your feedback orientation. This takes time, and also requires that you have a growth mindset – you believe that you can grow, learn, and change (Dweck, 2006). While you develop your feedback orientation in the long term, you can adopt three very specific mindsets "in the moment" of any feedback exchange.

Assume positive intent. One strategy that you can use to stay open and objective in dialogue is assuming positive intent (Barnes, Bullard, & Kohler-Evans, 2017). Assuming positive intent means approaching any interaction believing that the other person has good intentions. The assumptions that we make about others' intentions or motivations color our perceptions of their behavior. If we assume ill-intent, we automatically have our guard up, might get defensive, and are skeptical of the other person's words and actions. We enter a self-protective mode. For many, providing feedback to others can be an intimidating and uncomfortable experience. Because of this discomfort (and perhaps also a lack of skill or preparation), the feedback provider may not state the feedback completely clearly, or show the right degree of empathy or concern. They might talk too much – making the message unclear or digging themselves into a hole. They might fill silence with words that add no value. It's easy to interpret awkward behavior like this as uncaring or aggressive. However, if you assume positive intent, you give the feedback provider the benefit of the doubt, that they really do care and are just doing a bad job giving you the feedback. Remember that the other person may feel uncomfortable – and they are putting themselves into this uncomfortable position *because* they care about you and want to help you learn, grow, or uncover a blind spot. The truly uncaring person is the one who *doesn't* go out of their way to give you the feedback.[3]

Understand what is happening in your brain. You are hardwired to have an immediate emotional reaction to negative feedback. "Cool cognition" and rational thought take time to catch up with "hot emotion." Give yourself time to let the immediate emotional reaction pass before you can truly process and think clearly about the feedback. The sooner that you recognize this, the easier all of your feedback interactions will be. Mindfully processing the feedback that you receive is the gateway to doing anything productive with it (London & Smither, 2002). The amount of time that you need to get past your emotions and really process the feedback may vary based on the feedback, the situation, and your own patterns and tendencies. Simply counting to ten may provide the time and space that you need to be able to process feedback. Perhaps you need more time to process and the best course of action for you, for the feedback provider, and for ensuring productive outcomes is to say, "Thanks. I need to give this a little more thought. Do you mind if we reconnect later today or tomorrow morning to talk more about next steps?" Don't be afraid to be candid: "This is a lot to process and I feel like I need a little time and space to reflect on this feedback." Once the emotion has passed and you're able to think more clearly about the feedback, you don't just have to blindly accept it. You have a range of choices in how you will handle the feedback.

In addition to understanding the role of emotion, cognition, and biology, remember that the attitudes and beliefs that you have developed over the course of your lifetime also affect your feedback experiences. Your overall attitude toward feedback – your feedback orientation – underlies how you feel about feedback (Do you love it? Hate it?), how much you value feedback, if it helps you gain self-awareness, if you find it useful for growth or improved performance, and if you feel accountable to do something with feedback you receive (Linderbaum & Levy, 2010). Your feedback orientation will affect the mindset and attitude that you bring into a feedback interaction, how you initially react and respond to the feedback, and what you choose to do with it. Although your feedback orientation has been shaped by years of past experiences, you can choose to invest in and develop your feedback orientation by learning to value, use, and seek it out. Although many aspects of our personality and who we are as people are relatively stable over time, we can shift our attitudes and beliefs. Openly accepting feedback and using it to have higher performance will help you build self-efficacy and self-confidence over time, which, in turn, will make you more open to and assured about handling feedback in the future (Brown, Ganesan, & Challagalla, 2001; Colquitt, LePine, & Noe, 2000). Your current mood can also impact how you perceive feedback. The congruence or incongruence between mood and feedback sign determines how people react to

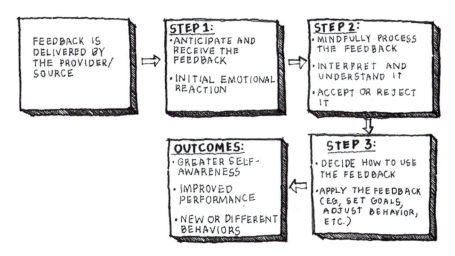

Figure 5.2 Accepting and deciding to use feedback is a multistep process! (Adapted from London & Smither, 2002).[4]

feedback. Feedback is more likely to be viewed as accurate when the sign of the feedback is congruent with the recipient's mood. In a negative mood, we view negative feedback as more accurate and are more inclined to process it deeply; in a positive mood we view positive feedback as more accurate (Hammer & Stone-Romero, 1996).

Take ownership for your 50% of the interaction. Feedback is not a one-way dialogue (although many people seem to have the misconception that it is). Although it may feel like the feedback provider is in full control and feedback is "happening to you," remember that you are 50% of the dialogue. The three behaviors that follow provide specific actions that you can practice, but ultimately *success begins with you seeing yourself as an equal participant in the dialogue*. Research has shown that feeling a sense of ownership for their work (or whatever the target/focus of the feedback) leads people to be more open to asking for feedback (Qian, Lin, Han, Tian, Chen, & Wang, 2015). Only you "own" your behavior, and have the ability to choose what actions you will take based on the feedback you've received. Even if the person giving you feedback is in a significant position of power or authority, or if the feedback feels extremely high-stakes, you always have a choice. The choice is much broader than "just accept it as is" or "outright reject it" – there are many shades in between. You can use the three behaviors described next to assert your 50% of the feedback exchange and make any feedback dialogue feel more productive.

Behaviors

Once your mind is in the right place, you can choose how you want to engage in the feedback discussion. If the feedback provider is highly skilled at delivering feedback, the next steps may seem clear and you will walk away feeling supported, encouraged, and with tangible next steps for action. However, if the feedback you receive is not entirely clear, provokes you, feels inconsistent with your own perceptions, or otherwise raises questions, you have many tools available to help you to make the most of the interaction. Empathy goes a long way on both sides of the feedback exchange. On the receiving end of feedback, you want the feedback provider to show empathy in their delivery of the feedback. As a feedback recipient, you can use empathy to better understand where the feedback provider is coming from should you not entirely agree with their feedback. Try to take their perspective – what are they seeing that you are not seeing? How has their experience of the focal situation differed from your own? It's easy to get caught in the trap of wanting to be "right" (or being sure that you are "right"); don't let your need to be right get in the way of understanding the other person's perspective. And it's impossible to truly understand the other person's perspective if you aren't really listening to them.

Really listen. In Chapter 4 we learned about the importance of being fully present and *really* listening in order to be an effective feedback provider. Listening is equally important when you are on the receiving end of feedback. Listening to understand – not to react or respond – will enable you to gain a deeper understanding of the situation and what the other person is trying to tell you. Think about a recent experience that you had as a feedback recipient. When the person providing feedback to you was talking, how deeply were you listening? Were you practicing open and objective listening, attempting to really hear and understand their feedback? Or were you simply "reloading" and thinking about all the things that you wanted to say in response –either to prove why you are right and they are wrong, or to rationalize your behavior or explain why that situation was a one-off exception? If you are thinking about how you want to respond, you are not truly listening. You are engaging in "level 1" listening, which is completely self-focused. Taking your listening to "level 2" means hearing what is being said, and also what is not being said; it is listening with empathy and to truly understand the other person's perspective (Whitworth, Kimsey-House, Kimsey-House, & Sandhal, 2009).

Failing to pay full attention will lead to you missing subtle nuances in their words, tone, expressions, and body language that serve as important data points in the dialogue. In order to listen at this level of depth, you must be mentally present in the conversation. Distractions such as technology or focusing on your "inner monologue" will inhibit you from being fully present and listening at this level of depth. If you find yourself getting derailed by your own reactions to the conversation (e.g., feeling like feedback is unfair, disagreeing with a statement), use your powers of curiosity and empathy to stay focused. Practice empathy and expand your understanding by considering possibilities like, "I wonder why she feels that way?" or "How could he be seeing this situation differently than I am?" Listening carefully for the answers may help you stay present and focused in the discussion and not get distracted by your own inner monologue and immediate reactions.

Ask Questions. Questions can be your secret weapon in a feedback conversation. Questions not only invite more information and clear up potential confusion or misunderstanding, they can also help you buy time and manage your emotions in a challenging feedback discussion. For example, during Rae's annual performance review, her manager gave perplexing feedback: "Rae it's been a tough year and this just isn't working." Rae's immediate reaction was one of surprise and alarm – her feedback throughout the year had never led her to believe that things "weren't working." Rae felt her heart rate increase, her palms begin to sweat, and her mind start to race ("I'm not performing. I'm going to get fired. OMG I don't want to look for a new job. What happened?"). She took a few deep breaths and said to herself, "I have no idea what she means – before I freak out let me see what I can figure out." Rae asked her manager, "Lee, can you tell me more? What exactly isn't working?" Rae pulled herself back from her emotional downward spiral and asked open-ended questions to draw out her manager. As the conversation unfolded, Rae discovered that it wasn't as bad as she had thought. Her manager, Lee, was referring to one specific project where a complex team structure was holding back progress. But Lee kept most of the context in her mind and started the feedback conversation with vague, general, sweeping feedback – quite the opposite of the specific, behavior-based feedback that actually drives learning and performance.

In this example, Rae's manager, Lee, failed to use feedback best practices. Rae could have let her immediate assumptions, reactions, and emotions take over and derail the conversation, but instead she exerted her 50% ownership of the dialogue and asked open-ended questions to help Lee more effectively express her feedback. Open-ended questions are essential to move feedback discussions forward. Unless the feedback provider is a true expert at providing feedback, who practiced and prepared for the conversation, it's likely that they will unintentionally leave out some information, gloss over a few important details, or fail to provide sufficient context. As a feedback recipient, you can choose to simply accept the feedback exactly as it is provided, despite potential holes, lack of clarity, or open questions. Alternatively, you can choose to actively engage in and advance the dialogue by asking clarifying questions, asking for examples, or inviting more information. Coaches use open-ended questions (e.g., what, how, when questions; even "tell me more") to draw out their coachees and develop a full picture of the situation. As a feedback recipient, you can borrow this coaching strategy in order to get your own full picture of the feedback. Remember, the person providing feedback to you may be deeply uncomfortable and have difficulty fully explaining the issue. By asking them open-ended questions you will put them at ease, better understand the situation yourself, and change the tone of the conversation from potentially contentious or awkward to productive and collaborative.

Look toward the future. As we learned in Chapter 2, one way to make feedback feel more constructive, to make the recipient less defensive, and to truly drive better future outcomes is to make it forward-looking. As the feedback recipient, you cannot control whether or not the feedback provider makes their feedback forward-looking. Their feedback may be entirely backward-looking, which could lead you to feel powerless, deflated, or defensive. After all, if the conversation is entirely focused on past events, there is no way to remedy the situation or change what has already occurred. However, as an active participant in the feedback exchange, you can ask a simple question to flip the lens of the feedback. In Rae and Lee's conversation, for example, Rae could ask "Going forward, how can we change the composition of the team to improve the trajectory of this project?" or "What role can I play in this project going forward to get it back on track?" This shifts the focus of the conversation away from rehashing the past and what's not working with the team, and into a creative problem-solving mode. Discussing future behavior (either by asking a question or suggesting what you will do in the future) also shows the feedback recipient that you have heard and understood their feedback, and are already thinking about ways to act on it. Despite being backward-looking, the real value of feedback is to help people to engage in more effective future behaviors.

Make the Most of Formal Feedback

Much of this book has focused on informal, day-to-day feedback; feedback that is provided between individuals during the course of work and daily life. In my list of 25 instances of feedback that I recorded in a single day (Chapter 1), you may have been surprised by how basic and mundane most of the examples were. If so, you're not alone. Most people, when they think of feedback, think of formal, "event-based" feedback – such as an annual performance appraisal (DeNisi & Pritchard, 2006; London & Smither, 2002; Pulakos & O'Leary, 2011). I have a bias toward day-to-day, informal feedback. It tends to have less buildup, feels like less of a big deal, can be delivered in a timelier manner, and is more likely to take the form of process feedback (as opposed to outcome feedback; from Chapter 2), which more easily leads to action and behavior change. Many of the same feedback best practices apply in formal feedback settings, along with some other situation-specific considerations.

Performance reviews. Formal feedback can be a valuable source of information, and the experience of receiving it can feel different from day-to-day informal feedback. Annual performance reviews at work are a prime example. Feedback provided in annual formal conversations looks more like outcome feedback. It tells the recipient a summation of their performance for the year and it is likely to be tied to important administrative processes like compensation, promotion, and annual goal setting. Receiving negative feedback in a performance review can be challenging because the opportunity for redemption may not exist. Let's go back to our example of Rae's performance conversation with her manager, Lee. If Rae received a "Needs Improvement" rating, sure she can make huge strides in the year to come, but that will not undo the disappointing rating that she received this year, which is likely now in her employee record for the foreseeable future. Looking back to Chapter 2, we learned that negative outcome feedback like this is the least likely to drive any future feedback seeking or performance improvement. In a disappointing formal review, emotional reactions may be even stronger. For instance, in a study of their performance management process, researchers at Adobe (2017) found that 34% of millennial employees cried after their performance review and 47% started looking for new job opportunities.

Emotional reactions to formal events like annual reviews may be more extreme (stronger negative emotions in response to disappointing reviews; stronger positive emotions in response to exemplary reviews), but many of the same practices still apply for maximizing the feedback dialogue – such as truly listening, asking questions to clarify and understand, and looking ahead to the future. These strong emotions take time to pass, so a follow-up conversation a few days or weeks later to discuss next steps and implications can be effective. After an exemplary, positive review, it can be tempting to bask in the glow of the great feedback and rewards, but once that initial glow has passed, try to think mindfully about how high performance can be repeated (or accelerated) in the year to come. Remembering that you are 50% of the feedback exchange is important for formal reviews, too. Research has shown that people have stronger negative reactions to performance reviews when they feel that they were not actively involved in the process (Cawley, Keeping, & Levy, 1998).

360 feedback. Surveys and assessments also provide valuable formal feedback. Many organizations use 360 feedback assessments to help employees get a holistic picture of their behavior or performance and how they are perceived by others, such as leaders/managers, peers, direct reports, and clients. These raters are typically invited to provide anonymous feedback that is aggregated and compared to self-ratings on the same dimensions. Numerically rated questions (e.g., on a 1–7 Likert rating scale, for example) on a 360 may tie back to an organizational leadership or competency model, and also include open-ended questions where raters can provide qualitative feedback on what's working and what the individual could be doing better.

360 (or "multisource") feedback provides a reality check by comparing our self-perceptions with the perceptions of others. Research has demonstrated an inverse relationship between performance and self-ratings, such that high performers tend to underrate their abilities while underperformers overestimate their abilities (Atkins & Wood, 2002). 360 feedback is a uniquely valuable form of feedback that enables individuals to examine their self-perceptions up against the perceptions of others, often through visuals like bar charts or graphs that highlight disconnects. The gaps between self-ratings and others' ratings highlight important differences in what people think of themselves and how they are showing up to others. It could be that they behave differently with certain people or in particular situations, or that their self-perceptions are harsher or more lenient than others' perceptions. Gaps such as these that are surfaced in 360s open important doors for developing better self-awareness.

Participating in a 360 feedback assessment can drive higher performance, under the right conditions. Not surprisingly, behavior change and improved performance are most likely to occur when a 360 report contains a few specific, negative, behavior-based pieces of feedback (Smither & Walker, 2004). Receiving a large quantity of negative feedback, however, can feel overwhelming and lead to a decline in performance following the 360. Large quantities of predominantly negative feedback leave the recipient feeling deflated, demoralized, and unsure where to begin. Or, as Otis Redding put it in "Sittin' on the Dock of the Bay," "I can't do what 10 people tell me to do, so I guess I'll remain the same" (Redding & Cropper, 1968).[5]

Certain characteristics or individual differences of the feedback recipient make behavior change more or less likely, as well. A 2005 meta-analysis of longitudinal multisource feedback studies found that improvements in performance are most likely to follow 360 feedback when the recipient has a strong feedback orientation, believes that they can change,[6] perceives a need for change, is high on conscientiousness (one of the Big Five personality variables),[7] and is goal oriented and effective at setting goals (Smither, London, & Reilly, 2005). Changes in behavior and performance following 360 feedback tend to be gradual and incremental; sufficient time should pass before doing a follow-up assessment.

360 feedback allows participants to calibrate their behavior against others' standards, but the feedback provided by ratings alone may be insufficient. Ideally, qualitative feedback or comments in the 360 report help to explain some of those gaps, but will rarely be exhaustive. When participants in a 360 receive their feedback report, they may be tempted to quickly scan over it, looking for surprises, dimensions where they are rated highest, as well as the biggest gaps between their self-ratings and others' ratings. But even the shortest 360 report is dense, with rich data points reflecting many perspectives, and may raise more questions than it answers. To extract the most value from a 360 report, an individual may want to give it a read, then put it away and look at it again a few days later with fresh eyes. An individual's mood and mindset at the time of reading the report can influence their perceptions of the feedback and what they take away from it. Rather than being an "end product," a 360 feedback report is best considered as the starting point for important follow-up dialogue. This is where the importance of asking directly for feedback enters the picture.

Ask for It

People proactively ask for feedback for a variety of reasons and generally weigh the costs and benefits before asking (Ashford & Northcraft, 1992). They may genuinely want useful, constructive feedback to help them identify ways to improve their performance (aka an "instrumental motivation" for seeking feedback). They may have an ego-based motive: They want positive feedback to feel better about themselves. Sometimes people seek feedback to enhance their image, in an attempt to look good in front of others (Ashford, Blatt, & VandeWalle, 2003). Similarly, they may avoid asking for feedback as a means of self-preservation or ego defense, particularly in the presence of others. They don't want to risk looking foolish or uncertain in front of others. Regardless of their motive, feedback seeking puts the feedback recipient in the driver's seat, allowing them to control who gives them feedback, where and when they receive feedback, and the focus of the feedback.

Recent research has shown that shifting the directionality and ownership of feedback exchanges in the workplace, from being provider-driven to recipient-driven, makes the exchange less stressful for both giver and receiver (West, Thorson, Grant, & Rock, 2018). West and colleagues found that giving unsolicited feedback resulted in higher anxiety and heart rate for both giver and receiver. However, when control over the feedback exchange was placed in the hands of the recipient (e.g., feedback was only provided when the recipient asked for it), both giver and receiver experienced less stress, a lower heart rate, and a friendlier feedback exchange. These researchers suggest that by inviting the feedback provider to give feedback, the feedback recipient is "breaking the ice" and creating a more collaborative, open dialogue for feedback.

Several conditions increase the likelihood that people will actively seek out feedback. As we learned in previous chapters, most people are very uncomfortable receiving feedback in public. The same goes for feedback seeking: People are significantly more likely to ask for feedback in private settings (Williams & Johnson, 2000). Even if they have the intention of asking for feedback, once people enter a public setting they will reconsider their intention and either modify their question or hold back entirely. They weigh the costs and benefits of asking for feedback, and consider the possible negative impact on how they will be perceived by others by asking for feedback. "Will I appear unsure, insufficient, or foolish if I ask this question?" People are also more likely to ask for instrumental feedback (that is, feedback to help them improve their performance, not just to make them look good or feel good) when they are working on something new, something that involves uncertainty, or when in the midst of change (Ashford et al., 2003).

Not all sources are created equal when it comes to asking for feedback. Feedback is much more likely to be accepted when it comes from a trustworthy and credible source. When the feedback recipient decides who provides feedback, they get to be selective and to focus on sources who have cultivated trust and credibility with them. Supportive, transformational leaders are significantly more likely to be asked for feedback than their more transactional counterparts (Levy, Cober, & Miller, 2002). A leader who only provides critical feedback without the foundation of a trusting relationship may soon find their direct reports actively engaging in "FAB" – feedback avoidance behavior (Moss & Sanchez, 2004).

Feedback seeking isn't always this overt. You may not realize that you engage in a subtle form of feedback seeking every day. "Monitoring" is a form of feedback seeking where individuals do not actively ask for feedback, but pay close attention to others' behavior and comments to pick up on feedback about their own performance and behavior (Williams & Johnson, 2000). David, the musician and producer we met in Chapter 1, uses monitoring extensively in live performances:

Live performances are a total feedback festival. If things are going well on tour and in live shows, you go out on stage and receive massive positive feedback from hundreds or thousands of people showing that they appreciate your work. Body language is such valuable feedback – you can say any words but your posture and your body really tell the true story. We've had shows where the crowd is looking at their phones or you see a lot of folded arms, talking, or a couple yawns, and it's pretty tough. That's when you realize how much you depend on that unspoken feedback from the crowd to perform.

After reading Chapter 1, did you pick a day to notice all of the feedback exchanges you encountered? How many examples of monitoring did you include? Directly asking others for feedback can be a more direct, efficient, and certain route for feedback, and monitoring can provide some cues and clues to help us to adapt our behavior and to shape the questions that we want to ask.

Feedback in the Palm of Your Hand

By proactively asking others for feedback you can lay the foundation for an effective feedback exchange. You can choose the context for the feedback. You can choose to ask in person, on the phone, or in writing in order to control the medium. You can ask in public or in private. You can ask immediately after something happens, or wait until you're ready and have some distance from the event. You can ask questions that invite behavior-focused (as opposed to YOU-focused) and specific feedback. You can evoke future-focused feedback by asking questions like "What's one thing I should do differently next time?" The simpler and more specific your question is, the easier it will be for the other person to respond. Remember, feedback providers may be just as intimidated and uncomfortable as you are. You can make feedback feel more comfortable and manageable for them by asking clear and focused questions.

When it comes to being a great feedback recipient, stay open and seek to learn and understand the other person's perspective. Listen, ask questions, make the most of the exchange, even if the other person botches it. But, ultimately, YOU decide what to do with the feedback they provide. You are 50% of the feedback exchange, and once feedback is given to you, you own the next steps. Accept feedback with grace, give yourself time to really process it, and then choose the best course of action to help you learn, grow, and achieve higher performance.

Try It

Today or tomorrow, ask someone for feedback. Ask anyone, about whatever is on your mind. Ask a colleague, a friend, your partner, your kids, a fitness instructor. Ask for feedback in a way that makes it easy for them to respond, and increases the likelihood that you'll get useful feedback in return. Feeling uninspired? Try this feedback fill-in-the-blank:

> [*Person's name*], I'm looking for some feedback on [*my performance, a project, last night's dinner, my tennis backhand, whatever*]. If I were going to do [*that same thing*] again tomorrow, what's one thing that you suggest I do differently?

Looking for More?

If you thought that this book would give you all of the secrets to organizational performance management processes you are probably really disappointed by the mere mentions of formal feedback and annual reviews. However, you will find great value in *Transforming Performance Management to Drive Performance* by Rose Mueller-Hanson and Elaine Pulakos (2018), two industrial/organizational psychologists who have extensive experience designing, implementing, and researching innovations in performance management.

Notes

1 An internal locus of control means that you believe that you can control your experiences and what happens to you. Having an *external* locus of control means that you believe that things are happening to you and are out of your control. An internal locus of control has consistently been linked to positive outcomes – such as success in school and work, an achievement orientation, better health, higher self-confidence and self-esteem, and seeing a direct effect between your hard work and effort and desirable outcomes, among other things.

2 Here, "mindsets" refers to the beliefs, attitudes, and expectations that influence how we perceive our experiences. In her work on "mindset," Carol Dweck (2006) focuses specifically on growth versus fixed mindset, which is an example of one set of attitudes or beliefs that people can have about their abilities.

3 Certainly, there's always a chance that you will encounter a selfish or deviant colleague or friend who *does* intend to harm or make you feel bad with their feedback. When you encounter them, consider asking yourself what is driving their ill intentions? Is

it about you, or is it really about them attempting to exert power, make themselves feel better or superior, or projecting from some other interaction? Approaching these interactions from a place of empathy and seeking to understand will help you to navigate them without surrendering your own power in the interaction.

4 Permission to include adapted figure obtained from Elsevier.

5 '(Sittin' On) The Dock Of The Bay'. Words and Music by Steve Cropper and Otis Redding. Copyright (c) 1968 IRVING MUSIC, INC. Copyright Renewed. All Rights Reserved Used by Permission *Reprinted by Permission of Hal Leonard LLC.*

6 Specifically, they have a strong incremental Implicit Person Theory, which means they believe that people are capable of change (similar to a growth mindset from Carol Dweck's 2006 research).

7 The Big Five theory of personality is one of the most widely used and accepted models of personality. In addition to conscientiousness, the Big Five traits include Neuroticism/Emotional Stability, Extraversion/Introversion, Openness to Experience, and Agreeableness (McCrae & Costa, 1987).

CHAPTER 6

USE IT

During my teacher training my small group of teachers were experts in offering fantastic, constructive feedback in the most caring way possible. I grew so much in the two weeks I spent with them. I'm the teacher I am today because of their guidance and feedback.

Parker, yoga studio owner and teacher

Without friends' and fans' encouraging feedback, Goodloe, who has painted murals all over the USA and captures the character, personality, and emotions of his subjects in his watercolor and acrylic paintings, would not be the professional artist he is today.

I only got started drawing and painting by posting little doodles and sketches online for fun. But people gave me reinforcing feedback – I like that a lot, do more, I want to see more of X. My art career was actually born out of feedback from other people. The encouragement I got from others, some of whom were total strangers, totally shaped what I'm doing now.

Without feedback from others via social media, Goodloe may not have realized that there was an appetite and demand for his work. He chose to listen to that feedback, to leverage it to propel his artwork forward, to a point where now it's not just for fun – it's actually his career. At the same time, he cautions against over-indexing on feedback from others.

> To wake up and say I need to create something so I can post it online and have something for people to react to can also be a bad thing – measuring the quality of your work based on the likes and comments you get on social media. I don't want to just create art that everyone likes. Only getting positive feedback can make you complacent and stop striving to grow and evolve what you are doing. Knowing that my work is always evolving allows me to incorporate feedback into whatever I will do next. I appreciate all feedback. Not getting reactions on your work from other people is like playing guitar alone in a dark room – you aren't going to get very far.

Generally, people give feedback because they want to see you do more of some behavior, less of another behavior, or some other behavior entirely. They are comparing your current behavior to some goal or standard – which could be explicit (an expectation they and/or you are aware of) or implicit (some expectation in their mind). As a feedback recipient, you ultimately have a choice about what you will do with feedback. When feedback is positive and indicates that you are doing great work or are on track with goals and expectations, you're less likely to be faced with a decision. You'll probably feel a shot of self-esteem and confidence in your work, then go about your business. People adapt very quickly to good news or gains, and then quickly revert back to "normal."[1] Negative feedback, however, presents you with a choose-your-own-adventure model – with many options for how to respond to the feedback and what to do with it (Taylor, Fisher, & Ilgen, 1984). After receiving negative feedback (and getting through your immediate emotional reaction), you could choose to accept it at face value and immediately put it to use by adjusting your behavior. You could opt to dig deeper on it to understand the real issues by asking questions or asking others for their perspective. You could simply choose not to accept it. Or you could think about it for a while and decide later. Even in situations where you may feel like you don't have a choice but to accept the feedback, you always have a choice about what to do with it.

Deciding What to Do

Chapter 5 emphasized that the feedback recipient is 50% of any feedback exchange. When someone provides you with feedback, you "own" the decision about what to do next. Some situations may feel more empowering than others – when your iPhone gives you feedback about your screen time, you might feel more discretion about what to do with that feedback compared to high-stakes performance feedback from your boss. But, ultimately, you have a range of choices about what to do next.

If you find the feedback to be accurate, helpful, and specific enough to imme- diately put to use, you may feel comfortable accepting it outright. For example, negative process feedback – that which tells you something you can do better or differently to get closer to your goals – can be applied right away and allow you to adjust or course correct in whatever you are working on (Earley, Northcraft, Lee, & Lituchy, 1990; Medvedeff, Gregory, & Levy, 2008). Many feedback exchanges are not so straightforward and simple, however. You may need time and space to overcome an immediate emotional reaction and think mindfully about the feedback, or you may need to ask follow-up questions to really under- stand the issue, why it matters, and what you will do about it.

Christopher, an alumni team member of the nonprofit Back on My Feet, has learned with time how to manage his emotional reactions to feedback. He has learned to find great value in feedback which in the past he would have simply reacted to and disregarded.

> With my training, I've learned that I get to decide in a situation what I will do with feedback from others. I've learned that I have more options than just reacting. Instead of responding with frustration and anger I can step back and make a conscious decision about what I want to do with the feedback. I've realized that I need to take time and recognize my feelings, not just immediately react because 9 times out of 10 it would be a negative reaction – a fight or flight response. I take a pause to practice empathy. I recognize that I don't always know what is going on with the other person, what they might be dealing with that I can't see. I recognize that they are human, too.

Taking the time to pause, let an immediate emotional reaction pass, and think mindfully about the feedback will also help you to identify missing pieces or fol- low-up questions to make the feedback more useful and more easily translated to new behaviors. Kluger and DeNisi's (1996) Feedback Intervention Theory (FIT) points out the importance of *levels of abstraction* in order for feedback to translate to meaningful behavior change. In a nutshell, we operate and adjust our behavior at very low levels of abstraction. When very high-level feedback is provided (e.g., a high level of abstraction), or that feedback prompts reflec- tion on the self, as opposed to on our behavior (e.g., person-focused feedback), translating that feedback into behavior change is difficult. Asking questions that drill into more specific behaviors and actions will identify specific ways to implement feedback, get closer to attaining goals or meeting expectations, and really understand what the issue is.

Another way to assess the value and relevance of feedback is to ask for additional opinions or find additional evidence to support or negate the feedback. One reason 360 feedback assessments are so valuable is because they offer an array of perspectives and do not over-index on one voice or one person's perspective. If someone provides feedback and you aren't sure if it's warranted, accurate, or useful, find some other people that you trust and ask for their opinion. Research has shown time and again that feedback is deemed more valuable when it comes from a credible source – someone who the recipient believes knows what they are talking about (has expertise on the issue) and is trustworthy (Albright & Levy, 1995; Ilgen, Fisher, & Taylor, 1979; Taylor et al., 1984; Vancouver & Morrison, 1995). Leverage your best practice feedback-seeking skills by asking open-ended, specific questions that enable others to feel comfortable giving you specific, constructive feedback.

Getting additional opinions or looking for patterns in feedback can provide a balanced perspective and ensure that the feedback is not simply a reflection of one person's preferences or expectations. For example, Alex, the restaurant manager we met in previous chapters, pays close attention to customer reactions, behavior, and feedback anytime a new dish is on the menu.

> If a dish is not finished or pushed to the side, we always ask for feedback on it. The absence of feedback is also meaningful because people usually comment positively on the dishes they love. So, if people are consistently NOT saying good things about a dish – that's meaningful feedback. It's not impressive and memorable enough. We look for patterns, and ask ourselves, is this feedback a one-off and simply attributable to one person's preferences? If I hear the same comment three times, that is meaningful, and we will act on it.

In Alex's example, calibrating the feedback is what ultimately drives her team to use or ignore feedback. If several different customers say that a dish is too salty, the kitchen accepts that feedback and adjusts their level of seasoning. However, if the guest at Table 20 believes the dish is too salty and everyone else who eats the same dish that night raves about it, the kitchen rejects or ignores the feedback from the guest at Table 20. Deciding what feedback to take on and what to ignore can be challenging. It requires some level of calibration and also a frame of reference for where the other person is coming from. In Chapter 1, David shared the example about another musician who he consistently disagrees with. When that friend gives feedback that he doesn't like something new that David plays for him, David actually knows he's on track. Although David is essentially rejecting the friend's feedback, he is able to interpret it as positive feedback since he knows they don't see eye-to-eye.

Choosing to accept and to act on feedback opens a whole new door of additional goal setting, behavior change, adopting or abandoning of habits, self-reflecting, and even asking for more feedback to track your progress.

Close the Gap

In reading an early draft of this book, a friend told me I went too deep, too soon with control theory in Chapter 1. I valued her feedback and used it to edit but not eliminate the discussion of control theory in Chapter 1, because I believe it provides a helpful way to break down and understand any situation that includes some kind of goal, behavior, motivation, challenge, and, of course, feedback. Feedback is more likely to be accepted when we think it has informational value that will help us to close the gap between where we are and where we want to be (London & Smither, 2002; Taylor et al., 1984). According to control theory, feedback is exactly the information that tells us the gap between where we are and where we want to be. Applied to some of the examples shared earlier in this chapter:

- In a successful restaurant, the goal is for guests to leave happy and satisfied with their experience. You want them to enjoy every dish that they eat (goal/desired state). If the **current state** of their experience is dissatisfaction with an overly salted dish, their **feedback** on that dish helps the kitchen to identify the gap between the current state and the goal state. Based on their feedback (aka "the comparator" in control theory), the action required to **close that gap** is adding less salt to the dish.
- If David's **goal** is to produce excellent music that he feels good about and his fans enjoy (goal state), and his **current state** is the sound of a new song he wrote, negative **feedback** from a friend whose feedback is usually *wrong* suggests that David is moving in the right direction – his new music will likely **achieve his goal** of a great new album that fans will enjoy.

Box 6.1 Distinctions

In helping clients to reframe or articulate challenges, a coach may push a client to make *distinctions*. Distinctions enable us to tell one thing apart from other, related things (Flaherty, 2010). Making distinctions between two very different things is easy. If you have a basic understanding of fruit, you can make distinctions between apples and oranges. You can eat the skin of apples, they are usually red or green, and have a crisp texture. Oranges must be peeled to be eaten, they are typically orange in color, and have a juicy, pulpy texture. The more expertise we have on a topic, the more precise our distinctions become. Sticking with our fruit example, an apple farmer will be able to make much more specific distinctions between types of apples, or the ripeness of an apple, than a typical consumer. If an apple farmer and I are both tasting Gala, Honeycrisp, and Fuji apples, the apple farmer will be able to pick out more, and also more specific, differences between the three. I, on the other hand, would probably just think all three apples were delicious and that one is bigger than the others and another has more of a pink tone than the others. Distinctions enable us to get the root of a challenge or problem that we are trying to solve. In the context of feedback, the ability to make distinctions can help us to hone in on the specifics of what we are observing. A leader with deep expertise on a topic will be able to discern distinctions in an employee's work that the employee may not notice. Specific feedback from someone with expertise can help others to learn about the nuances of their behavior and to develop new distinctions of their own. Distinctions also enable behavior change by helping us figure out exactly what we need to do differently and why. For example, if a golf coach gives you feedback on your swing, making a distinction between swinging from your shoulders versus swinging from your core can provide a breakthrough for a developing golfer struggling with their swing. By suddenly understanding the difference between swinging with their arms versus swinging with their torso, this developing golfer can now see clearly what they have been doing wrong and what they need to do differently on every future swing. They have a new distinction that they can use to adjust their behavior going forward.

When feedback illuminates a gap between a current state and a desired state, there are actually two ways to close that gap. One obvious choice is to adjust the current state to get closer to the goal or desired state. If Jose has a goal of getting As in every class this year, but his midterm report shows that he is tracking toward mostly Bs, one way he can close the gap is to strengthen his study behaviors for the second half of the term. He can make sure that he attends every class, stays totally present and engaged in every class, takes great notes, completes all of his reading and homework, and asks the teacher for additional support where he needs it. Alternatively, when feedback shows a gap, we also have a choice to stick with our current behavior and adjust the goal or desired state. In Jose's example, he could say, "Actually, I feel like I'm working really hard at school and doing everything I can. Maybe it's not realistic to strive for all As this year," and adjust his goal to a mix of As and Bs.

Goal setting theory has consistently shown that difficult, specific goals drive higher performance (Locke, 1968; Locke & Latham, 2002). Challenging goals "pull" our behavior to higher levels and drive us to exert more effort than easier or "do your best" goals. However, this effect depends on our level of ability and, also, our commitment to the goal. If you set a goal that you simply do not have the ability to achieve, it is unrealistic. Similarly, if you set a goal that you aren't truly committed to, you will not have the motivation and the drive needed to achieve it. Thus, if feedback highlights a gap between our current performance and a challenging goal that we don't have the ability or commitment to achieve, adjusting the goal state is likely a healthier and more productive alternative to ramping up our efforts.

Last year, two of my nieces set their annual goals for selling Girl Scout cookies. Nowadays, Girl Scouts have the ability to set their goals online, without necessarily running them by their parents first. One of my nieces set an ambitious sales goal of 90 boxes of cookies. Her younger sister went in a different direction, with a goal of selling eight boxes of cookies. Once the disparity of their goals became apparent, the older of the two decided to revise her target to 50 boxes (still a lot more than eight!). Some social comparison and reflection on her commitment and ability to sell 90 boxes suggested that her goal was a little *too* challenging. She also took stock of her sales opportunities – counting up family members and neighbors that she could sell to. Comparing her goal against another outside standard – her sister's goal – provided feedback on her initial vision, which drove her to do some additional fact-gathering and calibration and, ultimately, to revise her goal to something more realistic.

Goal commitment impacts how people respond when feedback highlights a gap between the current and desired level of performance (Carver & Scheier, 1998; Johnson, Chang, & Lord, 2006; Vancouver, 2005). If my niece had been deeply committed to her goal of selling 90 boxes of Girl Scout cookies, rather than adjusting her sales goal she would have adjusted her behavior. She could have set up shop outside of a retail store or a location where she would get foot traffic, above and beyond the family members and neighbors she accounted for as likely customers. She could have persuaded her uncle to buy 25 boxes, rather than ten. But, because her commitment to sell 90 boxes was not that strong, a revised goal was more realistic.

As a higher-stakes example, a friend – we'll call him Mr. Y – shared a story with me about feedback that led him to modify his career goal. At the time, Mr. Y was working in a conservative manufacturing organization. He had climbed the ladder quickly and aspired to continue progressing. In a conversation about future leadership opportunities, he was told by his manager that he would struggle to join the executive team because other people thought he was "too gay" and that he made them uncomfortable. Mr. Y explained to me that he and his manager actually had a good working relationship, but that his manager tended to be very blunt, but well intended, in her feedback. Knowing this, Mr. Y let his immediate emotional reaction pass, and asked her to "say more" about what exactly the issue was. He would have been justified in merely rejecting the feedback, given that it was deeply unfair, discriminatory, and generally bad feedback (vague, person-focused, not constructive, not actionable). However, being the confident, growth-oriented person that he is, Mr. Y wanted to understand what specifically it was about his actions and behavior that led her to make this blanket statement. He dug deep to understand the feedback and, ultimately, chose to adjust his goal from progressing in that organization to progressing in general in his career. Mr. Y soon departed the organization for a major promotion at another, more welcoming organization where he's seen great success, but not before seeking opportunities to learn and grow from even that most unproductive feedback. He owned the experience, letting his emotional reaction pass, asking questions to really understand the issue, and used the feedback to adjust both his goal state (overall career progression in his industry) and his current state (a new job in a new organization). Ultimately, that feedback did lead to a smaller discrepancy between his current and goal states – but in a different and more productive context.

Sometimes, adjusting our behavior to close the gap between current and desired behavior is hard, not because of lack of motivation, lack of ability, or excessively difficult goals, but because we have competing goals. In their meta-analysis of the impact of technology on behavior change, Hermsen and colleagues (2016) found that feedback generated by technology can be highly effective for closing gaps tied to behaviors such as eating less, eating better, exercising more, losing weight, and reducing water and electricity consumption. They also found that feedback will not lead to behavior change when another competing goal is present. For example, if your energy bills suggest that you are consuming a large quantity of hot water each month, and you care about conservation, you may cut back on long, hot showers or your use of hot water consuming appliances. However, if you have another goal of having extremely clean and sanitized clothing and dishes – and you are more committed to that goal than your conservation goal – you will likely not change your behavior. Your cleanliness goal essentially supersedes your conservation goal. The feedback on your energy bills may have increased your awareness of how much hot water you are consuming, but will not drive behavior change if you have another competing goal that is no more important to you.

When competing goals like this surface, you can choose to do nothing and simply accept the gap between your current behavior and the lower-priority goal, chalking it up to the importance of your higher-order goal. You could find ways to adjust your behavior that do not impact the higher-priority goal. In the hot water example, you could cut your showers from 12 minutes to 8 minutes per day, reducing your hot water consumption without impacting your laundry or dishwashing habits. You could also expand your definition of conservation to reduce competition with your cleanliness goals – focusing instead on cutting carbon emissions by biking to work rather than driving, and feeling less guilty about your hot water consumption as a result. Another option is to simply abandon one of your goals.

Goal abandonment is another viable option when feedback highlights a gap between our current and our desired state. In their discussion of strategies for dealing with goal discrepancies, researchers Campion and Lord (1982) noted that goal abandonment is actually a very adaptive choice, but people are generally afraid to let go of goals, for fear of looking bad or feeling like they've

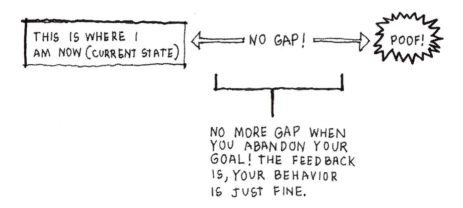

Figure 6.1 No longer a discrepancy when you abandon the goal!

given up. Hanging on to a goal that is no longer serving you, has no chance of being achieved, or is no longer relevant is completely unproductive. In instances like these, a moment of feedback can be a useful catalyst to pause and evaluate whether or not a goal is still worth pursuing, or if you should give it up and focus your time and energy on a goal that is more important or that you're more committed to.

Goodloe, the professional artist we met earlier, finds that abandoning or revising a goal gives him the freedom to truly create.

> Sometimes I will have a vision for what I want. I will paint this character and find that it doesn't match the expectation I had. I find expectations can be an enemy. Sometimes you have to start with what's there and let it develop, to exit the critical mode and pay attention to what's right in front of you. Letting go of expectations and the critical voice allows me to get into flow.

Although goal abandonment can be extremely practical as well as liberating, goal pursuit also helps us to close the gap between where we are and where we want to be. Changing behavior, adopting new habits, overcoming fears, and pushing oneself to higher performance are all challenging, and often very worthwhile.

Changing Your Behavior

When feedback highlights a goal-performance discrepancy (GPD), and we're committed to that goal and won't revise it or abandon it, it's time to get serious about the Big B – Behavior Change. If the ultimate goal of feedback is to drive some change in behavior – more of something, less of something, or something different entirely – this is where the magic happens, and also some of the biggest challenges. Translating feedback into new behaviors is not always straightforward and is often difficult. Behavior change requires strong self-awareness and an ability to see the nuances of our current behavior and how we need to adjust it. Behavior change also demands that we become aware of our habits and patterns, and do the hard work to modify them.

Two aspects of great feedback step into the spotlight when we move to making changes in our behavior: Specificity and a forward-looking frame. The more specific feedback is, the easier it is to identify the precise behaviors that we need to adjust (Ilgen et al., 1979). When feedback is forward-looking, we get a head start on figuring out what we need to change (Roberts, Levy, Dahling,

Riordan, & O'Malley, 2019). Backward-looking feedback puts the onus on the recipient to bridge the gap between what has been unsatisfactory in the past and what "better" looks like in the future. When feedback providers use the past as a data point to suggest what "better" looks like in the future, recipients are further down the path to adjusting their behavior toward "better." This is also why feedback dialogues, as opposed to one-way "transactional" feedback, are so helpful. If a feedback provider stops short of suggesting what could be different in the future, the recipient can simply ask the question, "What do you think I could do differently going forward?" or "If I were going to do this all over again next week, what does better look like?"

A control theory perspective suggests that we have one big goal driving our behavior – and we assess our current performance against that goal state. Although big, difficult goals are incredibly powerful for driving performance (Locke, 1968; Locke & Latham, 2002), smaller goals along the way can break down intimidating goals into manageable steps and also provide the satisfaction of achievement in shorter increments. We know from goal setting theory that failing to make sufficient progress can be a huge demotivator (Carver & Scheier, 1998; Johnson et al., 2006; Vancouver, 2005). Setting microgoals along the way enables us to track progress and to feel the motivational pull of satisfaction from achieving small milestones.

Most marathon training programs rely on microgoals to break down a big, daunting goal into manageable milestones. These microgoals keep training healthy and realistic. Instead of saying, "I'm going to go out and run 26 miles," marathon training programs have runners focus on incremental goals that gradually increase over the course of several months. A less experienced runner may begin with runs of two to three miles several days per week, eventually build up to long weekly runs of between ten and 12 miles, and, in subsequent weeks, runs of up to 22 to 24 miles. This slow build enables runners to feel a sense of achievement with each milestone, to develop their running condition and ability at a safe and healthy pace, and, ultimately, achieve their goal of running 26.2 miles. These incremental goals don't necessarily make goal achievement any slower – but they make it feel more manageable and with multiple milestones to continue driving behavior. As each microgoal is achieved, we get a burst of motivation and self-efficacy to carry on. As a runner in training proves to herself that she can run ten miles, she starts to believe that she can run a half marathon. As she surpasses 18 miles, suddenly 26.2 seem attainable. Microgoals provide mini control loops that provide feedback and gauge the distance to these small goals along the way to achieving the higher-order goal.

If you're really having trouble making change, implementation intentions take microgoals to the extreme. Implementation intentions help users to articulate exactly what they will do, when, and how. Typically, intentions translate to behavior change only 20–30% of the time (Gollwitzer, 1999). Implementation intentions are not just "good intentions," they are concrete, actionable plans that enable the user to take simple steps to get closer to their goals. They function as "if/then" statements, prompting the user to plan that when situation X arises, I will do Y (Gollwitzer, 1999). Implementation intentions can be especially helpful if procrastinating or struggling to get started on a new behavior is a challenge. For example, let's say feedback in your annual review suggested that you need to be a better listener. Your ultimate goal is to be a better listener. That's a big goal that requires some challenging behavior change. A microgoal could be to talk less and to listen more in each of your one-to-one meetings and calls at work. That's still a great intention, but breaking the habit of interrupting, taking up more "airtime" than others, or thinking about how you will respond instead of really listening is very challenging. Implementation intentions can help. In this situation, you might set the implementation intentions of, *when I'm on one-to-one calls with my direct reports and I feel the urge to*

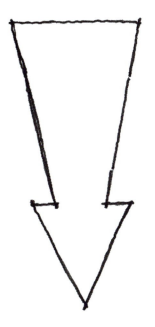

GOAL
RUN A MARATHON

MICROGOALS
WEEKLY MILESTONES -
3 MILES, 6 MILES, 10, 12,
18, ETC.

IMPLEMENTATION
INTENTIONS

WHEN I GET UP ON MONDAY,
WEDNESDAY, AND FRIDAY,
I WILL PUT ON MY RUNNING
CLOTHES AND COMPLETE MY
RUNNING PLAN BEFORE I GO
TO WORK.

Figure 6.2 Achieve tough goals by setting microgoals and using implementation intentions to get moving.

interrupt, I will pause and count to five before saying anything. Or, *I will open all of my one-to-one calls by first asking my direct reports what is on their minds and what they want to discuss on our call.* Implementation intentions work because they prompt the user to think through a future situation before it arises, and therefore to go into the experience more prepared, with a vision for how they will behave.

Self-awareness is key to effective behavior change. As you put feedback to work on making lasting changes in your behavior, develop a habit of pausing to reflect on what is working and where you are having challenges. What breakthroughs did you experience that make you feel excited and validated in your behavior change? What old habits, expectations, or situations are holding you back from making lasting changes in your behavior? What other goals are competing with your behavior change goals? Reflection is a critical component of behavior change that enables us to update our mental models and to incorporate new learning and experiences into our knowledge structures (Gray, 2007). Like visualization, reflection can reinforce and cement new attitudes, and attitudes that are developed with effortful thinking are more likely to translate into future actions and behaviors (Anseel, Lievens, & Schollaert, 2009; Petty, Wegener, & Fabrigar, 1997). Reflection on behavior change is even more powerful when it is coupled with … you guessed it … more feedback. Research by Frederik Anseel and colleagues showed that feedback is more effective for driving behavior change when it is coupled with reflection, and reflection is most powerful for driving behavior change when it is coupled with more feedback. High-impact behavior change comes about through an ongoing process of trying out new behaviors, pausing to reflect on the impact of those behaviors, and getting additional feedback to assess the impact of the behavior for closing in on goals.

Get Support from Others

Feedback is not a solo experience. Other people generously provide it, often despite their own discomfort. The way we respond to and use feedback impacts others. We also have the ability to enroll others to support us as we act on and apply feedback in our lives. 360 feedback assessments, which provide formal and very dense feedback, are most effective when the recipient works through the feedback with someone else, such as a professional coach. Researchers have found that working through 360 feedback with a facilitator or coach leads to setting higher development goals, creating specific action plans, and attaining higher subsequent performance (Seifert, Yukl, & McDonald, 2003; Smither,

London, Vargas, Flautt, & Kucine, 2003). Having an objective partner, such as a facilitator or coach, enables 360 recipients to be open and honest as they explore their feedback, to reflect on how their self-assessments differ from others' perspectives, and to plan – in a nonjudgmental environment – how they will follow through and take action on their feedback.

Adam, the Global Leader of Learning and Talent at a large multinational commercial real estate organization, shared an example of supporting leaders to make the most of a 360 feedback experience.

> We ran a development program where 100 of our top leaders participated in a 360 assessment. Typically, our feedback is very "behind the scenes" – we don't have a strong feedback culture, so I knew it was important to make them feel safe and supported for this experience to work. Participants attended a 2-hour workshop before they even received their assessment reports. We used what we know about psychological safety and set the tone that we all have strengths and also things that we can work on. We talked through the intention of the feedback, what to do with it, what to expect. We built trust with them and allowed them time to be nervous, to ask questions. We helped them navigate the feedback and figure out what to do with it. Many leaders came up to me afterward and told me it was the most impactful development experience of their career because they had never gotten feedback like that before – to understand how they are impacting others.

A 360 assessment is more likely to result in behavior change when users are held accountable for doing something with the results (Bracken & Rose, 2011). Organizations can boost accountability for using 360 results by providing support that helps users understand their feedback and set goals and intentions for follow-up. Offering this level of support for *all* feedback is unrealistic, though it would likely improve people's experiences of receiving and using feedback and strengthen their feedback orientation. Coaching and feedback go hand in hand, and not just for formal feedback processes like 360s. Coaches – whether professional coaches or simply managers, colleagues, or friends who use a "coaching approach" to engage (e.g., deep listening, asking open-ended questions, reflecting back what they are hearing) – can help others work through the feedback they have received, talking through initial emotions and reactions into creative problem solving. Coaches have a unique, objective position that enables them to "hold up the mirror" and provide feedback, help individuals self-generate feedback, and reflect on feedback others have provided (Gregory & Levy, 2012). Coaching, with its focus on behavior change, growth, and outcomes, is perfectly suited to helping people to do something with feedback, and to tie it back to their personal growth goals.

People who have a strong feedback orientation tend to be more open to coaching, *and* coaching can help to develop and strengthen feedback orientation over time (Gregory & Levy, 2012; Linderbaum & Levy, 2010).

Receiving feedback can feel lonely and isolating if it's overwhelming, challenges your self-perceptions, or is difficult to take action on. But, like asking directly for feedback, asking for support can eliminate some of the mystery and isolation. Asking for coaching support is one option, but support can also come from colleagues, friends, and family, as well as the person who provided the feedback in the first place. Following up and demonstrating accountability show that you have taken the feedback seriously. Letting the feedback provider know that you are doing something with the feedback can help to build your relationship and also strengthen their own feedback orientation because they can see that their feedback matters – that you are using it and doing something with it. Once they provide you with feedback, they are "in it" with you and, if you trust them and value their perspective, they can be a helpful source of support and thought partnership. Asking for additional feedback will not only help you to enroll the support of others, but it will also help you to track your progress as you make changes to your behavior and work toward your goals. As you work on new habits or behaviors, proactively seeking feedback from others lets them know that you are deliberately trying to change and gets them bought in to your development.

Embracing Your Inner Feedback Zealot

Deciding to love feedback is a choice. Even if you still struggle to give, receive, ask for, or use feedback, you can choose to embrace it and commit to developing your feedback orientation and to helping others to do the same. Feedback is so much more than formal "events" like performance appraisals, and shows up in every part of our lives – not just at work. Some of the most useful feedback is mundane and you may not even recognize it as feedback. We are constantly surrounded by data and information from other people, from our inner monologue, from technology, and from our environment that helps us to understand ourselves relative to the world around us. One goal of this book was to shift the way you think about feedback – where it comes from, what it looks like, how, and how often we receive it.

- How has your understanding of feedback evolved since you started this book?
- What did you learn about feedback that was most surprising?

- What were you already doing effectively in your own feedback practices?
- What ineffective feedback habits will you change as a result of what you have learned?

One way to become more comfortable with feedback is simply to use it more often. Try a 30-day feedback challenge and see how it impacts your comfort level with feedback. Every day for 30 days challenge yourself to give, ask for, and use feedback at least once per day. This exercise will make you more aware of the feedback around you, and also give you opportunities to practice, which is a critical part of behavior change. You can practice in any context – at work, with your family, your friends. Tell the barista at your local coffee shop that last time he filled your coffee to a point where you couldn't add cream and today could he please leave more room at the top – that's your feedback delivery for the day! Practice asking for feedback in a way that makes it easy for others to respond – open-ended, specific questions with a forward-looking frame. If you work in an organization, consider creating a 30-day feedback challenge for your colleagues. Share a tip on feedback best practices each day to develop others' feedback orientations and keep feedback top of mind.

We are immersed in a sea of feedback everywhere, all the time. Without it, we would wander aimlessly toward our goals, unsure of where we stand, what we are doing right, and where we are off course. Feedback is not only a valuable source of information, it's also a critical form of communication that – when given effectively – can build and strengthen relationships and connections, and – when given poorly – can undermine trust and chip away at relationships. Feedback can be challenging to give, accept, and use, but becomes more manageable when we apply what we've learned from behavioral science.

The beauty of these feedback best practices is that you can use them immediately. If you aspire to be better about giving feedback, but never get around to it, use what you have learned about implementation intentions to start doing things differently right away. Try this:

> Next time [situation where I want to provide feedback] arises, I will pause to think about the feedback I want to provide. I will plan what I will say, making it behavior based, specific, and forward-looking, I will say it, and I will stop, giving the other person time to process and respond.

Build your feedback-seeking muscles by identifying a goal you are working on that is important to you, and make a point tomorrow to ask someone whose opinion you trust for feedback on your behavior related to that goal. Try,

[*Person's name*], I am working to achieve [*your goal*] and want to get some outside perspective on how I'm doing. Based on what you've observed, what's one thing you think I'm doing that is helping me to get closer to that goal, and one thing you think that I could do differently or stop doing to help me to get closer to that goal?

Every time you give effective feedback, ask someone else for feedback, and pause to think about, accept, and find the value in feedback, you are strengthening your own feedback orientation and, possibly, the feedback orientation of whomever you're engaging with.

This book covered a lot of research and best practices. Below is my top ten list of favorite tools and practices:

1. Always focus feedback on behavior (or the task), not the person
2. Be as specific and evidence based as possible
3. Feedback is based on events that happened in the past, but we give it to drive future behavior. Give more effective feedback by making it forward-looking
4. Give feedback as soon as possible, but not in public and also not when you are emotionally hijacked
5. Take a moment to pause and choose the most effective medium for your feedback, based on the situation and the person you're giving feedback to
6. When you receive feedback, remember that you are 50% of the exchange – it's not happening *to* you
7. Increase the likelihood that others will give you useful, high-quality feedback by asking questions that are specific and forward-looking
8. Embrace negative process feedback. It is the most valuable for assessing the gap between our current state and our goals, and tells us how to close that gap
9. Listen deeply and ask open-ended questions; these will serve you well in nearly any interaction, whether you are giving or receiving feedback
10. Remember that all feedback exchanges are human interactions occurring in the context of relationships past, present, and future

What's on *your* feedback top ten list?

_____

Try It

Take on a 30-day feedback challenge! Every day, for 30 days, find an opportunity to give, ask for, and use feedback. Note how your comfort level with feedback changes over those 30 days. Keep it simple – these don't have to be intimidating conversations. Find meaningful small ways to bring feedback into your life. As you strengthen your feedback orientation, think of it as working out your feedback muscles!

Looking for More?

Behavior change is hard, and undoing old habits and adopting new habits can help. Both *The Power of Habit* by Charles Duhigg and *Atomic Habits* by James Clear provide accessible guidance and explanations for how habits form and how we can create new habits to support our goals and aspirations.

Note

1 Ask people how they feel and how their life will change after receiving a major promotion or winning the lottery, and they will grossly overestimate the impact of the news or gain. Research has shown that people experience a short burst of positive emotion immediately after the experience, but quickly revert back to "normal" – how they felt and behaved before the great event. This phenomenon is known as the "hedonic treadmill" (Brickman & Campbell, 1971).

REFERENCES

Adobe. (2017). *Performance review peril: Adobe study shows office workers waste time and tears*. Available at https://news.adobe.com/press-release/corporate/performance-review-peril-adobe-study-shows-office-workers-waste-time-and-tears.

Albright, M. D., & Levy, P. E. (1995). The effects of source credibility and performance rating discrepancy on reactions to multiple raters. *Journal of Applied Social Psychology, 25*, 577–600.

Alvero, A. M., Bucklin, B. R., & Austin, J. (2001). An objective review of the effectiveness and essential characteristics of performance feedback in organizational settings (1985–1998). *Journal of Organizational Behavior Management, 21*, 3–29.

Ammons, R. B. (1956). Effects of knowledge of performance: A survey and tentative theoretical formulation. *The Journal of General Psychology, 54*, 279–299.

Anseel, F., & Lievens, F. (2006). Certainty as a moderator of feedback reactions? A test of the strength of the self-verification motive. *Journal of Occupational and Organizational Psychology, 79*, 533–551.

Anseel, F., Lievens, F., & Schollaert, E. (2009). Reflection as a strategy to enhance task performance after feedback. *Organizational Behavior and Human Decision Processes, 110*, 23–35.

Ashford, S. J., Blatt, R., & VandeWalle, D. (2003). Reflections on the looking glass: A review of research on feedback-seeking behavior in organizations. *Journal of Management, 29(6)*, 773–799.

Ashford, S. J., & Northcraft, G. B. (1992). Conveying more (or less) than we realize: The role of impression management in feedback seeking. *Organizational Behavior and Human Decision Processes, 53*, 310–334.

Atkins, P. W. B., & Wood, R. E. (2002). Self- versus others' ratings as predictors of assessment center ratings: Validation evidence for 360-degree feedback programs. *Personnel Psychology, 55*, 871–904.

Au, A. K. C., & Chan, D. K. S. (2013). Organizational media choice in performance feedback: A multifaceted approach. *Journal of Applied Social Psychology, 43*, 397–407.

Bandura, A. (1986). *Social foundations of thought and action: A social cognitive theory.* Englewood Cliffs, NJ: Prentice Hall.

Barnes, C. D., Bullard, M. B., & Kohler-Evans, P. (2017). Essential coaching skills for affective development. *Journal of Education and Culture Studies, 1,* 176–185.

Bernstein, E. S., & Li, S. (2017). Seeing where you stand: From performance feedback to performance transparency. *Academy of Management Proceedings, 1,* 14752.

Bishop, J. (2013). *Examining the concepts, issues, and implications of internet trolling.* Hershey, PA: IGI Global.

Bodenhausen, G. V., Kramer, G. P., & Susser, K. (1994). Happiness and stereotypic thinking in social judgment. *Journal of Personality and Social Psychology, 66,* 621–632.

Bracken, D. W., & Rose, D. S. (2011). When does 360-degree feedback create behavior change? And how would we know it when it does? *Journal of Business and Psychology, 26,* 183.

Bracken, D. W., Timmreck, C. W., Fleenor, J. W., & Summers, L. (2001). 360 feedback from another angle. *Human Resource Management, 40,* 3–20.

Brickman, P., & Campbell, D. T. (1971). Hedonic relativism and planning the good society. In M. H. Appley (ed.), *Adaptation-level theory* (pp. 287–302). New York: Academic Press.

Brown, K. W., & Ryan, R. M. (2003). The benefits of being present: Mindfulness and its role in psychological well-being. *Journal of Personality and Social Psychology, 84,* 822–848.

Brown, S. P., Ganesan, S., & Challagalla, G. (2001). Self-efficacy as a moderator of information-seeking effectiveness. *Journal of Applied Psychology, 86,* 1043–1051.

Cabral, L., & Hortacsu, A. (2010). The dynamics of seller reputation: Theory and evidence from eBay. *Journal of Industrial Economics, 58,* 54–78.

Campion, M. A., & Lord, R. G. (1982). A control systems conceptualization of the goal-setting and changing process. *Organizational Behavior and Human Performance, 30,* 265–287.

Carver, C. S., & Scheier, M. F. (1998). *On the self-regulation of behavior.* New York: Cambridge University Press.

Cassidy, J., Ziv, Y., Mehta, T. G., & Feeney, B. C. (2003). Feedback seeking in children and adolescents: Associations with self-perceptions, attachment representations, and depression. *Child Development, 74,* 612–628.

Cawley, B. D., Keeping, L. M., & Levy, P. E. (1998). Participation in the performance appraisal process and employee reactions: A meta-analytic review of field investigations. *Journal of Applied Psychology, 83,* 615–633.

Chang, C. H., Johnson, R. E., & Lord, R. G. (2010). Moving beyond discrepancies: The importance of velocity as a predictor of satisfaction and motivation. *Human Performance, 23,* 58–80.

Cheng, J., Bernstein, M., Danescu-Niculescu-Mizil, C., & Leskovec, J. (2017). Anyone can become a troll: Causes of trolling behavior in online discussions. *CSCW: Proceedings of the conference on computer-supported cooperative work,* 1217–1230.

Clear, J. (2018). *Atomic habits.* New York: Penguin Random House.

Colquitt, J. A., LePine, J. A., & Noe, R. A. (2000). Toward an integrative theory of training motivation: A meta-analytic path analysis of 20 years of research. *Journal of Applied Psychology, 85,* 678.

Cooperrider, D. L., & Srivastva, S. (1987). Appreciative inquiry in organizational life. In R. W. Woodman & W. A. Pasmore (eds), *Research in organizational change and development* (Vol. 1, pp. 129–169). Stamford, CT: JAI Press.

Dalio, R. (2017). *Principles: Life and work.* New York: Simon and Schuster.

DeNisi, A. S., & Pritchard, R. D. (2006). Performance appraisal, performance management, and improving individual performance: A motivational framework. *Management and Organizational Review, 2,* 253–277.

Dominick, P. G., Reilly, R. R., & Byrne, J. (2004). Individual differences and peer feedback: Personality's impact on behavior change. Paper presented at the 19th annual conference of the society for industrial and organizational psychology, Chicago, IL.

Duckworth, A. (2016). *Grit: The power of passion and perseverance.* New York: Scribner/ Simon & Schuster.

Dweck, C. (2006). *Mindset: The new psychology of success.* New York: Random House.

Earley, P. C., Northcraft, G. B., Lee, C., & Lituchy, T. R. (1990). Impact of process and outcome feedback on the relation of goal setting to task performance. *Academy of Management Journal, 33,* 87–105.

Edmondson, A. (1999). Psychological safety and learning behavior in work teams. *Administrative Science Quarterly, 44,* 350–383.

Flaherty, J. (2010). *Coaching: Evoking excellence in others.* New York: Routledge.

Fox, S., & Duggan, M. (2012). *Mobile health 2012.* Washington, DC: Pew Research Center's Internet & American Life Project.

Fredrickson, B. L. (2001). The role of positive emotions in positive psychology: The broaden-and-build theory of positive emotions. *American Psychologist, 56,* 218–226.

Fredrickson, B. L. (2013). Updated thinking on positivity ratios. *American Psychologist, 68,* 814–822.

Gollwitzer, P. M. (1999). Implementation intentions: Strong effects of simple plans. *American Psychologist, 54,* 493–503.

Gray, D. E. (2007). Facilitating management learning: Developing critical reflection through reflective tools. *Management Learning, 38,* 495–517.

Gregory, J. B., & Levy, P. E. (2012). Employee feedback orientation: Implications for effective coaching relationships. *Coaching: An International Journal of Theory, Research and Practice, 5,* 86–99.

Gregory, J. B., & Levy, P. E. (2015). *Using feedback in organizational consulting.* Washington, DC: American Psychological Association.

Hall, D. T., Otazo, K. L., & Hollenbeck, G. P. (1999). Behind closed doors: What really happens in executive coaching. *Organizational Dynamics, 27,* 39–52.

Hammer, L. B., & Stone-Romero, E. F. (1996). Effects of mood state and favorability of feedback on reactions to performance feedback. *Perceptual and Motor Skills, 83,* 923–934.

Hays, M. J., Kornell, N., & Bjork, R. A. (2013). When and why a failed test potentiates the effectiveness of subsequent study. *Journal of Experimental Psychology: Learning, Memory, and Cognition, 39,* 290–296.

Hermsen, S., Frost, J., Renes, R. J., & Kerkhof, P. (2016). Using feedback through digital technology to disrupt and change habitual behavior: A critical review of current literature. *Computers in Human Behavior, 57,* 61–74.

Heslin, P. A., Latham, G. P., & VandeWalle, D. (2005). The effect of implicit person theory on performance appraisals. *Journal of Applied Psychology, 90,* 842–856.

Ilgen, D. R., Fisher, C. D., & Taylor, M. S. (1979). Consequences of individual feedback on behavior in organizations. *Journal of Applied Psychology, 64,* 349–371.

Ilies, R., De Pater, I. E., & Judge, T. (2007). Differential affective reactions to negative and positive feedback, and the role of self-esteem. *Journal of Managerial Psychology, 22,* 590–609.

Jawahar, I. M. (2010). The mediating role of appraisal feedback reactions on the relationship between rater feedback-related behaviors and ratee performance. *Group & Organization Management, 35,* 494–526.

Johnson, R. E., Chang, C., & Lord, R. G. (2006). Moving from cognition to behavior: What the research says. *Psychological Bulletin, 132,* 381–415.

Kabat-Zinn, J. (1994). *Wherever you go, there you are: Mindfulness meditation in everyday life.* New York: Hyperion.

Kauffman, C. (2006). Positive psychology: The science at the heart of coaching. In D. R. Stober & A. M. Grant (eds), *Evidence-based coaching handbook: Putting best practices to work for your clients* (pp. 219–254). Hoboken, NJ: Wiley.

Kluger, A. N., & DeNisi, A. (1996). The effects of feedback interventions on performance: A historical review, meta-analysis, and a preliminary feedback intervention theory. *Psychological Bulletin, 119,* 254–284.

Levy, P. E., Albright, M. D., Cawley, B. D., & Williams, J. R. (1995). Situational and individual determinants of feedback seeking: A closer look at the process. *Organizational Behavior and Human Decision Processes, 62,* 23–37.

Levy, P. E., Cober, R. T., & Miller, T. (2002). The effect of transformational and transactional leadership perceptions on feedback-seeking intentions. *Journal of Applied Social Psychology, 32,* 1703–1720.

Li, A. N., & Tan, H. H. (2013). What happens when you trust yoursupervisor? Mediators of individual performance in trust relationships. *Journal of Organizational Behavior, 34,* 407–425.

Linderbaum, B. G., & Levy, P. E. (2010). The development and validation of the Feedback Orientation Scale (FOS). *Journal of Management, 36,* 1372–1405.

Locke, E. A. (1968). Toward a theory of task motivation and incentives. *Organizational Behavior & Human Performance, 3,* 157–189.

Locke, E. A., & Latham, G. P. (2002). Building a practically useful theory of goal setting and task motivation: A 35-year odyssey. *American Psychologist, 57,* 705–717.

London, M. (2003). *Job feedback: Giving, seeking, and using feedback for performance improvement.* Mahwah, NJ: Erlbaum.

London, M., & Smither, J. W. (2002). Feedback orientation, feedback culture, and the longitudinal performance management process. *Human Resource Management Review, 12,* 81–100.

Luca, M. (2016). Reviews, reputation, and revenue: The case of Yelp.com. Working Paper: Harvard Business School.

McCauley, C. D., Lombardo, M. M., & Usher, C. J. (1989). Diagnosing management development needs: An instrument based on how managers develop. *Journal of Management, 15*, 389–403.

McCrae, R. R., & Costa, P. T., Jr. (1987). Validation of the five-factor model of personality across instruments and observers. *Journal of Personality and Social Psychology, 52*, 81–90.

Medvedeff, M., Gregory, J. B., & Levy, P. E. (2008). How attributes of the feedback message affect subsequent feedback seeking: The interactive effects of feedback sign and type. *Psychologica Belgica, 48*, 109–125.

Moss, S. E., & Sanchez, J. I. (2004). Are your employees avoiding you? Managerial strategies for closing the feedback gap. *Academy of Management Executive, 18*, 32–44.

Mueller-Hanson, R., & Pulakos, E. (2018). *Transforming performance management to drive performance*. New York: Routledge.

Northcraft, G. B., & Ashford, S. J. (1990). The preservation of self in everyday life: The effects of performance expectations. *Journal of Personality and Social Psychology, 40*, 521–531.

O'Malley, A. L., & Gregory, J. B. (2011). Don't be such a downer: Using positive psychology to enhance the value of negative feedback. *The Psychologist Manager, 14*, 247–264.

O'Malley, A. L., Ritchie, S. A., Lord, R. G., Gregory, J. B., & Young, C. (2009). Incorporating embodied cognition into sensemaking theory: A theoretical integration of embodied processes in a leadership context. *Current Topics in Management, 14*, 151–182.

Pat-El, R., Tillema, H., & van Koppen, S. W. M. (2012). Effects of formative feedback on intrinsic motivation: Examining ethnic differences. *Learning and Individual Difference, 22*, 449–454.

Petty, R. E., Wegener, D. T., & Fabrigar, L. R. (1997). Attitudes and attitude change. *Annual Review of Psychology, 48*, 609–647.

Pulakos, E. D., & O'Leary, R. S. (2011). Why is performance management broken? *Industrial and Organizational Psychology, 4*, 146–164.

Qian, J., Lin, X., Han, Z. R., Tian, B., Chen, G. Z., & Wang, H. (2015). The impact of future time orientation on employees' feedback-seeking behavior from supervisors and co-workers: The mediating role of psychological ownership. *Journal of Management & Organization, 21*, 336–349.

Ranard, B. L., Werner, R. M., Antanavicius, T., Schwartz, H. A., Smith, R. J., Meisel, Z. F., Asch, D. A., Ungar, L. H., & Merchant, R. M. (2016). What can Yelp teach us about measuring hospital quality? *Health Affairs, 35*, 697–705.

Redding, O., & Cropper, S. (1968). Sitting on the dock of the bay. *On the dock of the bay*. [Album]. Memphis, TN: Stax Records.

Roberts, A., Levy, P. E., Dahling, J., Riordan, B., & O'Malley, A. (2019). Feedback just ahead: The future of feedback is before us. Symposium presented at the 34th annual meeting of the Society for Industrial and Organizational Psychology, National Harbor, MD.

Rock, M. L., Gregg, M., Thead, B. K., Acker, S. E., Gable, R. A., & Zigmond, N. (2009). Can you hear me now? Evaluation of an online wireless technology to provide real-time feedback to special education teachers-in-training. *Teacher Education and Special Education, 32*, 64–82.

Rodgers, W. J., Kennedy, M. J., VanUitert, V. J., & Myers, A. M. (2019). Delivering performance feedback to teachers using technology-based observation and coaching tools. *Intervention in School and Clinic*, 55, 103–112.

Sapolsky, R. M. (1994). *Why zebras don't get ulcers: A guide to stress, stress related diseases, and coping*. New York: W.H. Freeman.

Scott, K. M. (2015). *Radical candor: How to be a kickass boss without losing your humanity*. New York: St. Martin's Press.

Seifert, C. F., Yukl, G., & McDonald, R. A. (2003). Effects of MSFB and a feedback facilitator on the influence behavior of managers toward subordinates. *Journal of Applied Psychology*, 88, 561–569.

Smither, J. W., London, M., & Reilly, R. R. (2005). Does performance improve following multisource feedback? A theoretical model, meta-analysis, and review of empirical findings. *Personnel Psychology*, 58, 33–66.

Smither, J. W., London, M., Flautt, R., Vargas, Y., & Kucine, I. (2003). Can working with an executive coach improve multisource feedback ratings over time? A quasi-experimental field study. *Personnel Psychology*, 56, 23–44.

Smither, J. W., & Walker, A. G. (2004). Are the characteristics of narrative comments related to improvement in multirater feedback ratings over time? *Journal of Applied Psychology*, 89, 575–581.

Sparr, J. L., & Sonnentag, S. (2008). Fairness perceptions of supervisor feedback, LMX, and employee well-being at work. *European Journal of Work and Organizational Psychology*, 17, 198–225.

Steelman, L. A., Levy, P. E., & Snell, A. F. (2004). The feedback environment scale (FES): Construct definition, measurement, and validation. *Educational and Psychological Measurement*, 64, 165–184.

Tadelis, S. (2016). Reputation and feedback systems in online platform markets. *Annual Review of Economics*, 8, 321–340.

Taylor, M. S., Fisher, C., & Ilgen, D. (1984). Individual's reactions to performance feedback in organizations: Control theory perspective. In K. Rowland & G. Ferris (eds), *Research in personnel and human resource management* (pp. 81–124). Greenwich, CT: JAI Press.

Tetlock, P. E. (1985). Accountability: A social check on the fundamental attribution error. *Social Psychology Quarterly*, 48, 227–236.

Ungerleider, S. (2005). *Mental training for peak performance: Top athletes reveal the mind exercises they use to excel*. Emmaus, PA: Rodale Press.

van der Kleij, F. M., Eggen, T. J. H. M., Timmers, C. F., & Veldkamp, B. P. (2012). Effects of feedback in a computer-based assessment for learning. *Computers and Education*, 58, 263–272.

Vancouver, J. B. (2005). The depth of history and explanation as benefit and bane for psychological control theories. *Journal of Applied Psychology*, 90, 38–52.

Vancouver, J. B., & Morrison, E. W. (1995). Feedback inquiry: The effect of source attributes and individual differences. *Organizational Behavior and Human Decision Processes*, 62, 276–285.

Vich, M., & Kim, M. Y. (2016). Construction and application of radical candor: Efficiency of criticism at work. *Central European Business Review*, 5, 11–22.

Waung, M., & Highhouse, S. (1997). Fear of conflict and empathic buffering: Two explanations for the inflation of performance feedback. *Organizational Behavior and Human Decision Processes, 71*, 37–54.

Weitzel, S. R. (2000). *Feedback that works: How to build and deliver your message.* Greensboro, NC: The Center for Creative Leadership.

West, T. V., Thorson, K., Grant, H., & Rock, D. (2018) Asked for vs. unasked for feedback: An experimental study. *Neuroleadership Journal.* Available at https://neu-roleadership.com.

Whitworth, L., Kimsey-House, K., Kimsey-House, H., & Sandhal, P. (2009). *Co-active coaching.* Boston, MA: Davies-Black.

Williams, J. R., & Johnson, M. A. (2000). Self-supervisor agreement: The influence of feedback seeking on the relationship between self and supervisor ratings of performance. *Journal of Applied Social Psychology, 30*, 275–292.

Wiita, N. (2018). Motivosity. In S. Young & C. McCauley (Chairs), User-driven leader feedback tools. Panel at the annual conference of the Society for Industrial and Organizational Psychology, Chicago, IL.

Yang, B., Watkins, K. E., & Marsick, V. J. (2004). The construct of the learning organization: Dimensions, measurement, and validation. *Human Resource Development Quarterly, 15*, 31–55.

Young, S., & McCauley, C. (2019). User-driven feedback tools for leader development. In L. Steelman & J. Williams (eds), *Feedback at work* (p. 265285). Cham: Springer.

INDEX